SPOKEN IN WHISPERS

SPOKEN IN WHISPERS

The autobiography of a horse whisperer

Nicci Mackay

MAINSTREAM
PUBLISHING

EDINBURGH AND LONDON

The moral right of the author has been asserted

First published in Great Britain in 1997 by
MAINSTREAM PUBLISHING COMPANY (EDINBURGH) LTD
7 Albany Street
Edinburgh EH1 3UG

ISBN 1 85158 942 2

A catalogue record for this book is available from the British Library

Typeset in Berkeley
Printed and bound in Great Britain by Butler and Tanner Ltd, Frome

Contents

1

To Tell or Not to Tell?

'Bear down, Nicci! Bear down! Now push, squeeeeeze with your thighs! Remember, bars of steel! Push now, bear down. How does it feel? Breathe . . . breathe, remember to breeeeeathe. Have you got him yet? Look! Look what he's doing.'

I didn't need to look, concentrating on gasping great lungfuls of air in as dignified a manner as possible; considering how he was feeling, he was doing fantastically well. At that stage, I was selfishly more worried about my lasting the course; yet another trickle of sweat was running down the centre of my back and collecting in a pool under my seat. The book on Emma's innovative riding technique had been difficult to follow, but nowhere near as difficult as her riding course was turning out to be.

Poise and tone, two of the most painful words associated with riding. Tone, they say, is required in order to ride with poise, hence the need for stomach muscles that would not flinch under the impact of a sledgehammer, and thighs that could squeeze the breath out of a rhino. All in order that one might float across the ground, totally in harmony with the horse, instead of being the more accustomed sack of potatoes tied to the saddle.

I had not really wanted to bring Arnie on the course with me. There had been an option to borrow a horse but, unfortunately, there had been a huge demand for places, and too few owners brave enough to lend their horses to unknown participants. I had therefore no real choice; forfeit the course – or go, in the hope that it wouldn't prove too much for Arnie.

I was there to learn to ride 'properly'. During my years in racing, I had been renowned for my 'stickability' and lack of fear. Since leaving the racing world, however, I had encountered successful and professional 'horsey' people from other disciplines; people who began to impress upon me the need to take control of my wayward mount, to ride with precision and in a polished style.

The general consensus of opinion was that Arnie had talent, balance and ability in abundance, and if only 'that girl' would get a grip of him, then he would definitely go a long way. My balance was considered good, and I had earned a reputation for being a natural with young or difficult horses, but, in the eyes of these others, I couldn't actually 'ride'.

Eventually, and unusually for me, I had become conscious of the opinions of this new equestrian fraternity, and I had believed them. Now, among skilled instructors with years of disciplined riding technique at their disposal, I hoped to master this new controlled approach.

However, I was struggling to come to terms with the whole philosophy of this, and so was Arnie. During his previous career as a point-to-pointer, he had been handicapped by a lung problem, in spite of an operation intended to help. He had also sustained various injuries, some of which he had never fully recovered from. As a result, I had never asked anything of him. My focus, when riding, had always been to take a back seat – to go with what I was given. If he marched along with a long springy stride, then that was marvellous. If he was having a stiff day, with his back and his joints aching, then we would stroll along gently, with me mirroring his lopsidedness. If we were jumping at breakneck racing speed, then I would just sit still and attempt to bring him back to me and steer for the next fence. I had never taken the driver's seat before in this way.

'Nicci! How are your tendons?' I was awoken from my daydream by a great booming, operatic voice. The woman must have had eyes in the back of her head, for I was not the only person in the arena at that moment; there were others, each of us undergoing our own personal masochistic session.

'Do they feel like knicker elastic yet? Bear down remember! Head up . . . and smile!'

I gasped. Smile? . . . *smile!* It was as much as I could do not to cry out in agony. I looked across and threw her a smile and a grunt as best as I could manage whilst gritting my teeth.

I most certainly was using muscles that had lain dormant for far too long, but at what cost? Would I ever be able to walk again when they winched me off? I could already feel my legs taking on the consistency of rubber and they had no body weight on them yet. Instead of the picture of grace and elegance that I was aiming for, I would have gone unnoticed lying in a field of beetroots.

And at what cost to Arnie? I knew the pressure he was under. I knew how he was feeling, both physically and emotionally. I struggled to pay attention to Emma, to hang on in there, battling with my guilt as it became increasingly difficult to come to terms with my dilemma: Arnie, despite his valiant efforts to cope with this new style, was being punished by pain as his muscles struggled to respond to the demands I was putting on him. Punished in spite of his courage, in spite of his attempts to give of his best.

'That's better, Nicci. Tone, remember, tone – back straight, seat bones down. Concentrate now, come on.' Emma was slight of stature, yet with a definite presence, as she boomed commands to all from the centre of the indoor arena. Clad in smart, khaki, cavalry twill jodhpurs and a head scarf, she conveyed and received respect.

My dilemma increased. We could not continue like this. I had to get Arnie out of here and back to the stable block. But how could I excuse myself? What reasonable explanation could I give for leaving in the middle of a lesson? It would seem so rude. To the external eye, Arnie looked magnificent; handsome, calm and poised – there were no outward signs of his suffering. What on earth should I do?

'Come on, Nicci! Pay attention, tits to his ears remember, tits to his ears!' In spite of everything, I had to laugh. Emma had the strangest expressions to explain what she wanted, but they certainly stuck in the mind! *Tits to his ears.* My old riding instructor in Germany would have had heart failure.

Without warning, Arnie suddenly spun around and took off across the arena, standing vertically on his hind legs, sending everybody scattering for cover. It was not the danger, more the speed and suddenness of his response that caught those on the ground unawares. The other horses being schooled took Arnie's actions as a cue for general 'freedom of expression time' and promptly started squealing, bucking and galloping around. The others were quickly brought under control but Arnie, who had now reached the limits of his endurance, stood straight up on his hind legs again, pawing at the air.

I was conscious of a sea of open mouths, somewhere far below my lofty vantage point. This was not the kind of behaviour one expected in the hallowed grounds of a dressage arena. 'Enough now, Arnie. You're out of order,' I spoke quietly but firmly to him as he reared again. I knew that what he was doing was not out of malice so I resorted to my usual method of sitting still and going with the flow. At that point all four feet returned to earth. 'Thank you,' I whispered.

'Oh well sat!' said Emma. There was a pause as our gaze met; the usual custom now was for 'loons' – as Arnie had now been branded –

9

to be schooled by Emma herself, or for her to offer tuition on how to deal with such a horse.

I looked her straight in the eye; there was no way that I was going to put him through any more. 'I'm going to put him away now, he's had enough for today, he feels too pressured, and his back is killing him.'

She looked surprised, and I was conscious of the silence and curious glances from the other riders and onlookers.

'Yes, yes, Nicci, you do just that,' came the reply. In normal circumstances one would have been expected to take control, to ride the horse through the problem and come out the other side triumphant. What I had said had registered, but made no sense. Emma then carried on with the others who had now all returned to their tasks.

Back at the stable block, which was empty apart from two other horses, I tended to my distressed horse. Trying to keep a handle on my emotions, I washed him down and put rugs on his trembling, breathless body, shivering in spite of the heat of the summer's day. I talked to him softly and told him not to worry. I was not at all ashamed of his behaviour, but I was ashamed of my own. All those times in the past, when we had muddled through in our usual slap-dash way, we had been together; he led and I followed, somehow knowing that he was doing his absolute best. But now I had taken over, using physical and mental force. And I had hurt him. Really hurt him.

As I allowed this realisation full throttle, I besieged him with a tidal wave of sobbing guilt, almost enough to wash him down all over again. What on earth had I been thinking of? Just because I had been humiliated by others into a submissive reappraisal of my riding, I had allowed myself to believe that I was letting Arnie down by not working him 'properly', allowed myself to believe that others knew my horse better than I did.

Guilt. I had been motivated to come on this course by guilt and, right now, I felt it – through every nerve-ending in my body. I was overwhelmed by huge waves of guilt, enveloped in it as if by a blanketing, moisture-laden, November fog.

I wept. Boy, did I weep – for him and for me. His back was so sore. I could feel great tearing pains racking through his shivering muscles. I could also see the beginnings of soft-tissue swellings rising under his silky coat; huge, hot and tender blisters. And all for what? Not for him, that was for sure.

I massaged him and fed him homoeopathic remedies, shovelling them into his mouth. Perhaps they would take this nightmare away. I was so consumed by my own self-punishment that I barely heard my name being called.

'Nicci?' Jackie, my room-mate, was standing behind me. 'Are you all right?'

My reddened eyes had obviously betrayed me. 'Yes, I'm fine thank you. I just feel so bad about Arnie.'

Jackie put her grey gelding away in his stable next door to Arnie. 'Your boy seemed a bit pressured before the end there. Is he going to be okay?' she enquired with genuine concern.

Just hearing those few words made me feel so much better. At least here was one person who was not going to brand my horse a 'head case' and me a wimp for not sorting him out.

'Yes, he's okay. I knew I was asking a lot of him.' My head spun. Dare I tell her? Dare I explain what had really happened?

I decided to say nothing. Robert, my husband, had warned me, as he'd dropped me off here, that I shouldn't expect to find people who would calmly accept that I communicated telepathically with horses. After all, *he* hadn't initially. He was probably right. How on earth could I ever explain to anybody what was going on; what I was capable of – what horses were capable of – without them all thinking me mad?

As we all left the yard at the end of the day, I stopped off in the village for some supplies on the way to the bed and breakfast lodgings. Such had been my hurry to come away on the course that I had arrived without any shampoo or deodorant, both of which I needed in abundance if I was to salvage something from my features in time to meet the others later for a drink in the local pub.

Fortunately, the little b&b where several of us were staying was only round the corner and I was first in. That meant – hot water! I ran myself a bath in the tiny bathroom, more of a 'sit-up-and-beg' type of bath, but one of the advantages of not being very tall is that these things don't matter. With the combination of a cup of tea, cigarette, steaming hot water and Radox, I was beginning to feel that I might be able to walk again after all. Gradually, as I was enveloped in the warmth of the relaxing water, I felt myself becoming dazed, my mind a whirl of mixed emotions and fears. I managed to still myself into a sort of dreamy half-world between asleep and awake.

There was a sharp tap at the door and I disappeared under for a fraction of a second, coughing great mouthfuls of bathwater as I emerged.

'Nicci! Nicci! Are you ready yet? We're all gagging for a drink now, and you've been ages!' yelled Jackie.

I looked at my watch; somehow I had lost an hour! Had they moved the clocks without telling me? Wide awake, I was dressed in a flash and followed behind them all to 'The Old Bull and Cow'.

Five of us had arranged to meet, to talk over the events of the day, and have something to eat. There were David and Marion who had travelled from the north of England to attend this course for the third time – real gluttons for punishment. The techniques I had found impossible to achieve at home with Emma's book, both Marion and David achieved with consummate ease. What was worse, they could both accomplish these near-contortions and still manage that elusive 'smiling' thing.

David was a keen intermediate dressage rider, tall and elegant; his horse a beautiful bay Hanoverian gelding called Flash who had a jet black mane and tail and seemed devoted to David. David was keen for the chiropractor who attended these courses to look at Flash's neck. Everybody knew that there was a problem somewhere around the neck area, but to date nobody had been able to find anything and it was stopping Flash in his work. Whilst David's vet couldn't find anything obviously wrong, he had no objections to Flash's being seen by a specialist as such.

Marion, David's wife, was prominent in the local hunt. Riding for her was very much a release from the pressures and strains of the environment in which she worked, and hunting was her pleasure, although her ambition was to perform a perfect dressage test. As with so many who ride to hounds, it was not the kill but the gallop across the moors in the company of others, feeling part of a team, that she so loved. She was a 'team' sort of person and enjoyed the camaraderie that belonging to the hunt gave her. Her horse was a chestnut Irish hunter-type gelding, called Flipper, 15 years old, and an ex-eventer.

Jane was a computer executive, whatever that meant. She tried to explain to me what she did at work but I'm afraid I go a bit fuzzy with techno talk. She certainly seemed high-powered and highly stressed accordingly, unable to sit still for any length of time without a glance at a clock or a watch. The time she spent with her horse was her 'quality time'; he was kept some miles outside London and she travelled for hours each day to and fro. Maddon, her Danish Warmblood, gleamed in appearance, almost black, with 'an eye for trouble and mischief', as Jane described him. 'If you're not careful to keep everything secure, he's off.' Maddon evidently had a knack, and passion, for opening stable doors; not just content with his own, he would delight in trying to open as many others as possible before being discovered.

Jackie was the fifth member of our group. This was the second time she had been on one of these courses and although she commented on how hard she found it, she felt her riding had improved considerably. I felt a great empathy towards Jackie; we shared a room because as smokers we felt ourselves to be outcasts compared with the others, and maybe fate had thrown the two of us together. I felt very comfortable talking to her about some of the things that I believed in, and she shared many of my views.

She had just resigned from a top marketing job in London to work with horses in a Swiss dressage yard for a fraction of the money. 'My family and friends at first found it quite hard to understand; after all I had at last become "successful". Why should I give it all up to go and work with horses? But as I used to drive everybody mad talking about horses all day, they were probably glad to get me out of their hair!'

I chuckled to myself for I knew exactly how she felt. I myself had followed the same burning ambition to work with horses all my life. It didn't really make much financial sense, but then there are thousands of other people passionate about horses doing just the same. Jackie had brought 'Robert', much to my amusement, only hers was much more handsome than my husband. Hers was a grey thoroughbred gelding, 16 hands in his stockinged feet!

'The Old Bull and Cow' was one of those lovely old, small, country-type pubs with beams and horse brasses, and a fireplace at each end of the room. There was a dartboard in the corner, a variety of odd-shaped tables and chairs dotted around the room, none of which matched, yet all fitted perfectly. It felt more like someone's front room than a pub. Various figures huddled around the tables in small groups and palls of pipe smoke filled the room from a lone figure sitting at the bar. He looked a regular with one of those comforting silver tankards, his name engraved proudly on the front. As we passed, his gaze caught mine and he winked and laughed. 'You lot must be over at Emma's, judging by the way you're all walking.' We groaned; was it that obvious that we'd all been tortured?

We chatted away about the day and how we all felt we were coping. It was good to see some progressing well, as it gave the rest of us, including me, encouragement to continue. It had been so hard for Arnie during the first day and I was still desperately worried about him. I didn't know whether he would want to try again tomorrow, it was up to him. I hadn't really had much chance at all to experience the 'feel' they were all talking about, but if Arnie couldn't face any more, then so be it. If he wanted to continue, then we would give it our best shot.

David, a doctor by trade and observant by nature, suddenly changed the tack of the conversation and asked about the deep scar on Arnie's underbelly.

'How on earth did you notice that?' I asked.

'Doctor's training I suppose. Anyway, it wasn't difficult to miss as you went past my nose with him standing up on his hind legs like that!'

I laughed; my father was an army doctor and equally observant. As children we could never manage to hide anything from him and every bump and scratch was examined in minute detail, followed by great tales of infection and pus, and how we must be more careful.

'That scar's seven years old now and the reason why I bought Arnie in the first place.' I was handed a steaming baked potato overflowing with beans and cheese. I thanked Jackie and we agreed to sort out the money once we got back to our room.

'Arnie was brought to me by a client who wanted him tidied up and sold,' I explained. 'His early career in steeplechasing had been marred, both because he was a very bad traveller which limited his choice of races, and also because of a wind problem he'd subsequently developed.

'They kept trying with him because of his good breeding. He had various operations to sort out his breathing problem, but to no avail. He still ran out of steam after about a mile and wasn't fast enough to be a sprinter so they brought him to me to sell on for another job. They pronounced him too "hot" to showjump, but too good for his current job as lead horse for the trekkers; he was destined for something in between. When he arrived he was aggressive in the stable, mistrustful and had a tendency to bolt.'

I paused as great shouts and cheers filled the room from the crowd gathered round the dartboard. Someone had obviously done better than expected.

'Carry on,' said Jackie, who had taken an instant liking to Arnie, as most people did, and wanted to know more.

I quenched my thirst on my 'medicinal' Guinness and continued. 'We were riding out one morning along one of the bridle paths close to the yard on the farm. I was riding Wellington, a thickset, Irish draught hunter, nearly as broad as he was long.'

'Where did he come from?' asked Marion.

'He belonged to another client who followed the local hunt. Anyway, Tina, the girl who worked for me, was riding Arnie as Wellie could be a bit of a handful at times. Arnie was getting really tense and uptight. As he started to rear and bounce around, Tina became nervous and started to clutch at the reins. "Drop your hands, for God's sake drop your hands!" I shouted, already seeing what was going to happen.'

'What on earth does "drop your hands" mean?' asked Jane.

'With a trained racehorse the more you take up the rein, the more you're telling it to get a wiggle on. Drop your hands and it should relax.'

Jane nodded in approval trying to work out in her own mind how Maddon would respond to such a command. 'What happened next?'

'Tina kept clutching the reins tightly,' I continued, 'and so Arnie launched himself and bolted along the path. I had to battle with Wellie to stop him following in hot pursuit, which would only have made matters worse. We followed sedately; me hoping that they would have stopped at the wicket gate at the end of the path. As I rounded the corner the sun was in my eyes but I was able to see the silhouettes of Arnie and Tina stopped some way ahead of us by the gate. I breathed a sigh of relief as I approached them.

'Then, as I moved nearer, out of the glare of the sun, the full impact of what had happened hit me. I could see that the gate was demolished with only the two support posts left standing. I flung myself from Wellie, and as I got closer I realised that Arnie was grotesquely crumpled in the middle of the splintered wood. His nose was on the ground on the far side of the smashed gate, where the narrow path inclined sharply uphill; forelegs folded under his chest, his hind legs were splayed out behind him at an unnatural angle. My mind spun and then I realised that he was actually propped up, impaled by a stake through the groin. At this point another horse and rider came up the track behind us; a friend. I yelled at her to call the knacker man – at this point I could see no hope for Arnie at all. "I'll call the vet," she said, disappearing off down the path.

'How could I get Arnie up? He was obviously in shock and completely stuck. There was no way he could get out of this alone. Totally on auto-pilot, I ran back to Wellie, grabbed my short racing whip, and dashing back to Arnie, I hit him – quite hard, three times – just above his tail, just where the central nervous system comes to a key point in the spine.

'It worked. On the third blow, he sort of sprang up – very quickly and easily, considering. I shouted to Tina to grab him, but being in a state of shock herself, she just stood there as Arnie galloped past, reins and stirrups flapping, blood and torn tissue trailing.

'It was a nightmare. Yelling at Tina to get back to the yard and stay there, I ran for Wellie, jumped on board and set off after Arnie. I was sick with fear. I tracked him across two fields following a trail of hoofprints and blood, imagining the worst as the trail took me on to what was, ordinarily, a busy country road.

'I dreaded what I might find, but to my relief I saw him, held by a lady who had stopped her car to catch him. Luckily Tina had followed us, taking a short cut across the fields, and was able to take Wellie from me. She set off back to the farm to get someone to bring the trailer.

'It seemed like an age before I heard the trailer coming. Arnie by now was beginning to sway slightly and I kept telling him to hang on . . . hang on, help was coming. Finally the trailer appeared round the corner, driven by old Owen who worked on the farm with Robert. Never was I more pleased to see his massive frame wedged in behind the wheel.

'With little difficulty we managed to manoeuvre Arnie into the trailer. By this stage he seemed almost too calm for my liking and I knew that he had lost a lot of blood. The journey to the surgery seemed painfully long and slow. They had been warned what to expect on our arrival so both vets were ready for us. They examined Arnie and sucked their teeth at what they saw. The stake had penetrated seven inches into his groin and yet miraculously had managed to avoid all his major organs.'

'He was very lucky,' said David. 'I've seen people in my time who haven't survived similar accidents.'

'The following two hours seemed to last a lifetime. They operated, allowing me to assist. They explained that they had done what they could for him, but that his chances of surviving the recovery period were slim. The wound was deep, he'd had a catheter inserted, and the likelihood of infection was high. I was allowed to take him home on the condition that I would phone them if he deteriorated at all.

'From that moment on, Arnie changed completely. All his aggression and mistrust towards me disappeared. He ate heartily, and would stand like a rock as I dressed his wound and sterilised the catheter. I was determined he wouldn't get infected so I rigged up a harness over his back to support a baby's disposable nappy to cover the wound, and this worked well.

'He began to regain his strength until the day came when I could turn him out in a field on his own; that was a special day for me. No one had believed that he stood much chance of survival, yet here he was now, bright as a button, cantering around the field.'

'So what happened with his owner? The guy who was trying to sell Arnie in the first place?' asked Jackie.

'Well, funny you should mention that. I actually bought Arnie before he'd even come round from the operation! I phoned my mother and begged her for the money. I can't explain it, but I just knew I had to buy him.'

I struggled to describe to these people how I really felt about Arnie, but the words were inadequate. 'I had never come across such presence in a horse, such courage, such reserves of inner strength. So I paid the owner the asking price. I also paid the vet's bills for making Arnie better. It was the best money I ever spent.'

As we left the pub for our b&bs everybody agreed that Arnie must surely be made of something special to be still alive today. We said our goodbyes and looked forward to another day of 'torture' back on the course.

Jackie and I returned to our room and decided to have 'one last cup of tea', which usually meant at least three or four!

'I was jolly impressed at how you managed to stay on board Arnie today,' Jackie said. 'Frankly, I don't understand what you're doing on a riding course when you can ride like that. You didn't budge an inch. I've ridden some pretty potty characters in my time but if it had been me, I'm sure I'd have come off. None of us could believe it when you just sat there and calmly told him that he was "out of order". Weren't you worried he'd go over backwards with you or something? He seemed pretty stressed out and that normally means fireworks.'

I groaned inwardly. Should I tell her? Would she really understand if I told her that the reason I was so calm at Arnie's apparent outburst was because I knew the cause? Because I knew that he was reacting to excruciating pain – pain that I had felt; because I knew how he was feeling emotionally; because I knew what his next move would be since I could catch his thoughts; because I knew he was a true and honourable friend and would never do anything to endanger me intentionally?

I brushed off Jackie's question. 'No, not really, I'm used to it.' Yet I felt I needed to talk to someone or I was going to burst. Before we had come, Arnie had told me that there were other horses apart from my own who needed my help, who needed someone to speak for them. The silent majority.

He had been right. The other horses somehow knew that I could hear them. David's horse had been the first, spinning me round and prodding me in the back of the neck, transmitting the pain so that it was replicated in minute and accurate detail in my own neck. My own horses would do this when they had a problem and now Flash was doing the same. *I knew where the problem was in Flash's neck but who was going to believe me?*

Jackie looked up from her mug of steaming tea and interrupted my train of thought. 'I overheard you telling Emma that Arnie's back was killing him just before you put him away. What did you mean by that? Does he have a problem?'

I paused for a moment, I was bursting to tell the truth and I felt somehow that Jackie would understand. I don't know why; it just felt right. I had told one or two people before and they had just either laughed or somehow felt threatened by what I was saying. Then, remembering Robert's warning, I decided against it.

'Yes, he has a few old racing injuries and finds some of the disciplined movements a bit too much to cope with.'

The conversation petered out slowly as the fatigue of the day caught up with us both. Giving in to our wearied eyelids, we headed for our beds.

2

Things Will Never be the Same Again

The following morning we were late to the stables but, with the help of several cups of tea and a cigarette or two, we managed to feed and muck out in time to finish with the others. After breakfast, I went over to Arnie and gave him a special hug. 'If you are sure you want to give it another try, we'll need to help each other today, my love,' I told him.

Once again we were working in groups in the arena, this time doing some work using trotting poles. As we waited for our turn I could feel Arnie becoming more tense. He knew that the lack of mobility in his back would prevent him from working over the poles to Emma's satisfaction, yet he wanted to try – to make amends for yesterday, to prove our worth, to show the others he was no 'nutter'. As he eyed the poles he tensed even more. I calmed him as best I could, telling him we had nothing to prove, that I would lead him away and we would forget the whole thing. He found this even worse; to fail without even trying would be too shameful for words.

'Trot him up, Nicci.'

This was our cue and we set off round the arena to approach the poles on the far side. I lined Arnie up, listening to my instructions as we started to turn into the line of six poles laid on the ground. Suddenly Arnie realised that, physically, he couldn't do it. This exercise demanded that he maintain a controlled rhythm in trot; he would need to flex his sore joints high enough to clear each of the six poles, to stretch his aching back and neck fully in order to keep his balance as he went down the line. He would not be able to make it and yet he couldn't pull out. His solution to the problem was dramatic; three strides and he was galloping, clearing the range of poles in one almighty leap reminiscent of his racing days.

Without a word I led him off and back to his stable. He was inconsolable. I spent a long time with him before I could bring myself to leave him and return to watch the others in the arena. What was I doing here? Why had I come? I had spent money I could ill afford on this course and all I had succeeded in doing was putting my beloved horse through the worst possible torment. I had placed him in an impossible situation. He was proud and sensitive and I had placed him in a position where he felt himself to be a failure.

Back at the arena, Jackie, once again, asked kindly after Arnie, remarking how impressed everyone had been by my tactful handling of him. But this was small consolation and, miserably, I took my seat to watch the afternoon's session.

During a lull in the proceedings, Jane got off Maddon to head for the loo and, asking if someone would hang on to him whilst she was away, ran off in a hurry leaving Maddon a little dazed in the middle of the school. He looked around and bypassing all those who reached out to take a hold of his reins, came straight to me.

He placed his great head in my lap. I knew what was coming. I had sensed it already. 'Help me.'

Cradling his head in my arms I felt a lump in my throat. A band tightened around my chest. I felt his despair, a great wave of hopeless despair. Arnie was right, after all, but what could I do?

Jane entered the arena again and laughed on seeing her horse's head in my lap. 'I never knew he could be so soft, sorry about that, hope he wasn't a nuisance.' As she mounted and rode away, Maddon caught my eye with a look that froze me to my seat.

Jackie's lesson on Robert had finished and she now joined me to watch the other group being put through their paces. David called out for some help with some awkward tack. As I left my seat to give him a hand with a buckle that needed smaller fingers than those he possessed, Flash grabbed me by my collar. With no intention of malice or danger towards me, he just held me to his chest and wouldn't let go, despite David's shocked attempts to release me. Eventually Flash relaxed his grip, my collar now well and truly sodden.

'I really am most dreadfully sorry. Are you all right?' David asked.

I laughed and explained that my own horses were always picking me up or sucking my clothes, and not to worry about it. 'I must taste nice to horses.' I returned to my seat as David rode away.

'You really do seem to have a way with them, don't you?' asked Jackie. 'Flash was so gentle then, he didn't seem to want to let you go, and I saw Maddon earlier on with his head nuzzling into your lap. What perfume are you wearing?' She grinned at me.

My head was spinning, I was getting more and more sensations coming from the horses. I had to do something or I felt I really would go mad. I decided to go for broke and, taking a deep breath, I blurted out, 'Jackie, what would you say if I told you that when a horse is in pain I can feel it in my own body?'

After a pause which seemed to last an age, Jackie replied, 'Well I'd say, "I wish I could do that."'

Her belief in what I had said, and therefore in me, was a tremendous relief. 'You're not laughing. Do you believe me? Do you believe it's possible?' I quizzed her rapidly for I could hardly believe the response I had received.

'Listen,' she said, 'I don't quite understand it all but I've seen enough over the past couple of days to know there's something different about what you are doing with horses compared with the rest of us.'

I could have hugged her; maybe I did, I can't remember. For years Robert had told me, and I had believed it myself, that should my gift become public knowledge I would be presented with a nice canvas jacket with sleeves which buckle up behind. So I had kept quiet. Now, at last, I had been given some confidence to talk openly about what I could do. Whilst Robert had been as supportive as he could, amazingly so considering his farming background, it meant a lot to me to talk to somebody 'horsey' about horses.

I knew Jackie was comfortable with what I had told her, but what about the others? And what about all the people outside this course? With a sinking feeling, I felt the confidence I had gained already draining from my system.

Jackie and I spent the rest of the day talking about my 'gift'; what I did, what horses sounded like, what they said, how they felt; she trying to convince me that I should speak up to the others; I, on the other hand, convinced it would be better to say nothing. After all, who was I to say to someone, 'I'm sorry your horse can't do what you are asking because it's in pain.' Who was I to speak up when a horse didn't understand the commands being given to it by its rider? Who was I . . . ?

'You must tell the others, Nicci, and tomorrow – they would all love to know.' Jackie was now putting on her authoritative voice. 'Well anyway, if you don't, then I will!' A shudder went through me. I knew determination when I saw it. I knew now there was no turning back.

The following day I turned Arnie out into one of the small paddocks behind the school. He had now stopped eating completely, such was his distress, and I hoped that a little fresh grass might tempt him. There was little more that I could do for him that I hadn't already done; he was a proud character, very 'old school', and he wanted to work this out his own way.

I returned to the indoor arena where the morning sessions were already starting, and took a seat in the viewing gallery. Emma was once again encouraging and praising her charges with enthusiasm. Each time Jackie went past on Robert, she mouthed something at me. I left my seat and moved closer to the front so that I might catch what she was saying. 'Have you told Emma yet?' she hissed. Another rotation of the arena and I gave my answer with a shake of the head.

'Seat bones, Jackie, seat bones! What are your seat bones doing? Where are they pointing now?' Emma had caught sight of poor Jackie 'slouching' as she would put it.

Jackie mouthed goodbye and set off diagonally over to where Emma was standing in the arena. From my vantage point I could see Jackie's position being adjusted in the saddle, a gentle pull here, a tweak there.

Emma's voice rose above the sound of the horses' heavy breathing and the squeaking of well-polished leather. 'Jackie! If your horse was taken out from underneath you, how would you land, on your feet or on your bottom?' I could see Jackie grinning as her position was readjusted again, being prodded and poked by Emma in places one really shouldn't expect to get prodded when learning to ride a horse! She set off once more.

'Better, Jackie, better.' She and Robert seemed to be going really well now and you could see quite a difference in his work and his carriage.

The lessons continued throughout the morning and with each session I found it harder and harder to concentrate on what Emma was saying. As the work grew more intense, I found myself picking up more and more information and sensations from the horses. Here came Flipper, and I felt the ligaments in my neck tighten like a vice, sending sharp shooting pains down the front of my chest. Watching Flipper and feeling his pains, I remembered the first time a horse had transmitted its pain directly to me. Prior to this occasion, I had only felt their pain when riding them, often assuming it to be mine.

If sound sleeping were an Olympic sport, I should certainly win a gold medal. My husband, Robert, teases me mercilessly about how impossible it is to wake me in the mornings. Yet one night last year I sat bolt upright in bed as if I had been prodded with one of those electric staffs they sometimes use for loading cattle.

My sudden movement shocked Robert awake. 'What on earth's going on? What's up, what's wrong?'

'I don't know, toothache I think,' I replied, startled at how awake I was.

Robert lay back again into his pillow; the lambing season was in full swing and he was dead on his feet. Muttering, he managed to ask whether I needed anything, without much intention of moving to get it – although it was the thought that counted. I lay down again and tried to go back to sleep. With each breath it felt as if my tooth was expanding in its socket and there was nowhere for it to go! Soon the whole of my jaw was throbbing. I sat up again and, leaving Robert to his slumbers, went downstairs for an aspirin, or a hammer, or something!

My sinuses were now filling and the pain in my jaw was moving to the front of my head as a dull aching sensation. I couldn't believe what was happening to me – I never got toothache. I stuck my fingers into my mouth to try to locate and soothe the offending tooth; goodness only knows what I was trying to do prodding and poking about, but I felt I had to do something. Ice, that would do the trick.

I opened the fridge to see a glacier forming where once the icebox had been. I found a large knife and chipped away at it, sending chunks of ice flying in all directions. One landed inside my T-shirt which made sure I was now wide awake. Eventually I managed to hack off a chunk to my satisfaction and held it gingerly to my jaw, the crystal melting gently as it touched my skin. As the ice-cold water trickled down my cheek and dripped onto the floor, I shivered with cold. I sat at the table with the ice clamped to my face but the throbbing would not subside and was joined now by a stabbing pain, as if a scaffold pole were being driven into my nerve by some great sledgehammer.

Then I thought of Arnie. I don't know why, or where it came from, I just felt I had to go and see him. Something was wrong. Dragging on my wellies and throwing a coat over my T-shirt, ice pack still clamped to my jaw, I hoped no one would see me as I padded down to the stables. 'Please don't let anyone be coming back from the lambing shed and see me like this.' I sped into the stable block where Arnie was kept; an American barn-type, all under cover and protected from the elements. The horses all stirred as I turned on the lights and stood blinking at me as they adjusted to the false glare. Almost unnoticed my toothache had gone. No longer was my head feeling as if it would explode, no longer my sinuses so tender to the touch. Arnie had achieved what massed bands in my bedroom couldn't; somehow, he had woken me from my sleep. He needed my help.

He stood in the corner with his head nearly to his knees, the side of his face swollen and his eyes sunken into his cheeks. A trickle of thick yellowish fluid was running from one nostril and his sinuses were impacted and tender. He looked a sorry sight. I searched in the tack room for the homoeopathic remedies I had been given for him the last time he had had trouble like this. I had been impressed with them then and, oh, so hoped that they would work again now. Bathing his face with cold water I waited for the tablets to take effect. Either as a result of the tablets, or the cold water, or having company, he seemed to buck up remarkably quickly, and soon I felt confident enough to leave him since he seemed so much more comfortable. In the morning I would call the vet to come out and see him.

'Nicci, would you like a go on Robert for a while?'

Jackie's voice started me from my daydream and I leapt at the chance, for I was still eager to see if I could catch up with the others in what they had achieved. Robert was so kind to me, letting me make my mistakes as I struggled to grasp the bare essentials of the technique. As I encouraged him more and more to show me what he had learned, he ended up teaching me! But then, that has always been the case with me and horses, and I have always felt that I have so much to learn.

As the lessons drew to a close for the day we waited eagerly for the arrival of Janice, the famed chiropractor, all of us hoping that she would be able to do something for poor Flash's neck. It was obvious from the way that he held himself, that something was stopping him from working, and Emma had gone to great lengths to reassure David that Flash was not simply just being evasive. She had ridden him herself and found him to be a most generous horse. As a result of his problem, all his work had been restricted to a walk instead of trot and canter until he could be sorted out.

As we waited for Janice's arrival, Jackie plied me with tobacco and wine. 'You will say something, won't you? You will tell her where the problem is?' More wine and more tobacco. I was not convinced at all that it would be a good idea. My nerves were as taut as telegraph wires. How could I possibly tell a professional that I knew better than they did within their chosen field of expertise and, moreover, that I had got it straight from the horse's mouth. I glugged back the wine; unusual for me but, right now, I needed something rather more fortifying than my customary tea.

Eventually a strange car drew into the yard which heralded Geraldine's arrival. She was a tall, elegant woman in her mid-forties, smartly dressed and well spoken – and very, very fierce looking. Jackie jabbed me in the ribs. I gulped and avoided her persistent glare. This woman was so efficient looking she was bound to find the trouble spot. Oh, *pleeease* let her find it!

'Right then,' barked Janice in the clipped precise tones of A Woman Who Stands For No Nonsense, 'where's the patient?'

We proceeded to the stables where Flash was waiting. Janice set about him with gusto, explaining as she worked what she was hoping to achieve, and what she felt was going on with him. As she worked away I could feel in my own neck the effects of what she was doing; quite spectacular really.

I nodded in approval as Jackie caught my eye to see how I thought things were going. 'Flash will be so relieved,' I thought to myself, 'just that last bit there, ooh, just there, no no, left a bit, just there.'

With that, Janice stopped. 'He'll be fine now,' she declared and moved off to the next horse. I was rooted to the spot.

As the entourage moved on to the next stable Jackie noticed the expression on my face. 'Whatever is the matter?' she asked.

'She's missed a bit, the most important bit. He's in absolute agony now; it's almost worse than before she started! Everything is stretched waiting for something to pop out but it hasn't.'

For a moment Jackie looked as shocked as Flash did. 'You must tell her then, and she will put it right.'

'I *can't* tell her! She wouldn't believe me, and anyway, do you know who she is?' I felt the colour draining from my face.

'That doesn't matter, you must say something. You *have* to,' Jackie urged me. 'You owe it to Flash if nothing else . . . to Arnie then, you have to say something – even if she thinks you're barking mad, you *must* say something! If you don't you'll regret it for the rest of your life!'

As we approached the group gathered around the next horse, I was surprised that no one looked round to see where the thumping noise was coming from. I thought my heart was going to beat out of my chest; my tongue had been replaced with a piece of dried, splintered wood and my legs had turned to jelly. We stood and tried to listen with interest as Janice proceeded to set about the horse in the next stable.

'Say something!' was whispered harshly into my ear. I tried to formulate a speech that would not offend but would make some sense. I was fumbling in my mind to think of the words when I was shoved in the middle of my back, and stumbled clumsily, falling almost at Janice's feet.

I looked up from my crouching position, my gaze working its way up the length of her well-cut trousers to the smart tweed jacket, and ending at her glare someway up in the heavens. Now I knew how Oliver Twist must have felt.

A silence descended. All eyes were on me. 'Excuse me,' I squeaked, 'I'm very sorry but you've missed a bit on Flash.'

'I've done what?'

I felt my cheeks getting hotter and hotter but I knew there was no turning back now. 'On Flash.' My voice was at least audible now. 'I can feel in my body what a horse feels, and you've missed a bit . . . sorry.'

Janice now announced to all within the next five counties what I had said. 'According to this young woman, she can feel what Flash is feeling and I have missed a bit on his neck that needs attending to!'

You could have heard a pin drop. Nobody knew what to say or do. We all stood staring at one another for what seemed a lifetime.

My heart was beginning to sink when Janice suddenly announced, 'Well, we had better take a look then, hadn't we?' She set off at a fearsome pace, but to her eternal credit, at least she was going to look, if only to dismiss what I had said.

I pointed to the spot on Flash's neck that was causing him the pain and we all waited. Janice set to work with her nimble fingers, exploring and cajoling, then she announced to the hushed multitude, 'And what's worse . . . she's right!'

I felt I was floating, I couldn't hear what anyone was saying as my mind blurred. 'You must speak out,' Arnie had told me, and I had. I felt his pride in me.

Jackie's face was beaming; the others around me registered the whole range – from bemusement through disbelief to outright shock. I thanked Janice for hearing me out, I owed her much. As she left, I was surrounded by the others, all eager to understand what they had just witnessed. Then I was led from one horse to another: 'Tell me about mine, how's mine feeling?' 'What about mine, what does he want?' 'How do you do it?' 'How long have you known?' These and a host of other questions I fielded as best as I could.

David came up quietly at the end. What I had done for Flash, he could not understand; it flew in the face of all his doctor's training. It made no sense to him, no logic at all, yet he had seen something with his own eyes that he couldn't explain. 'Thank you,' he stumbled over the words. 'Thank you very much.' We shook hands and parted; it had been quite a day.

As we settled back into our bed and breakfast for the night, Jackie and I were still chatting away. 'How exactly do you do it again?'

'Which bit?' I replied.

'The sort of talking thing you do with them. How does that work?'

I thought for a minute how best to explain it, but it wasn't easy. 'I get myself still, really still inside, slow everything down and then just wait and see what comes. Simple really.' Jackie laughed, and I said, 'Sometimes it comes as words, sometimes it's a series of images, sometimes it's very strong feelings, whatever is most appropriate.'

She sighed, not quite satisfied with my brief explanation. 'So then, when did you first find out that you could do all of this?'

'As a child really. I just thought nothing of it and assumed everybody could do what I do. As a child you don't question that you might be any different from anyone else. I suppose it's only in the last couple of years I've really set about trying to get to grips with it properly.'

It must have been the early hours of the morning before we finally fell asleep. I felt as if the weight of the world had been taken from my shoulders. I couldn't believe what had happened, and I couldn't wait for the next day to begin.

We were due to leave for home that day after lunch. I spent the morning with Arnie, talking to him and grooming him slowly, getting him ready for the journey ahead. A face popped over the stable door to see what I was doing. This was Sarah, one of the assistant instructors. I had been warned not to say anything to her; she had a reputation for being sceptical about anything 'alternative' and would not take kindly to anything I might say.

'I hear you can do funny things with horses, then; would you like to come and look at mine?' I was unsure if this was a challenge, or a request for help, but either way I agreed to visit.

I was led to the field where Sarah's horse was kept and was immediately struck with a feeling of despair. 'He's just not been himself lately, I can't put my finger on it, but all his sparkle has gone. I think it could be because I've just bought a youngster and he might be a bit jealous. Can you ask him for me?' She was looking furtively around to see if anybody was watching the two of us together, although I was a bit taken aback at how open she actually was.

I went over to her horse and gently stroked his muzzle, listening to what he had to say. 'Are you planning a big trip somewhere?' I asked Sarah.

She looked startled. I told her, 'He's worried if you will be all right on your own without him and also what will happen to him whilst you're gone.'

She now looked horrified. 'I've been offered a job in New Zealand! How do you know that?'

I looked again at her horse, and she too stared intently at him now. 'But how does he know? How do *you* know?' Sarah was trying to

27

understand as best she could. She could cope with thinking he did not like the idea of another horse, or even that he was worried she would ignore him in favour of the new arrival. But she couldn't understand how he knew that she was planning to go away, or that he cared for her, and cared about what she was going to do. I left her hugging her horse, shaking her head in disbelief.

Back at the yard, lorries and trailers were beginning to make their way homewards. Amid the goodbyes people came to thank me, wish me luck, ask last-minute advice. I was amazed, astounded and, oh, so grateful for all the support given to me. After years of guarded silence, it was wonderful to be able to speak freely, and to other 'horsey' people; and they wanted to hear what I had to say – what their horses had to say. Emma, in particular was very encouraging and it meant a lot to hear her tell me to 'go for it'. One lady took both my hands in hers and gave them an extra hard squeeze. 'It's a God-given gift, Nicci,' she confided. 'You must make sure that you use it.' I nodded and smiled, yet another lump in my throat. All this emotion was becoming too much to handle.

With that my mood was shattered as my husband Robert appeared, driving into the yard in a very different vehicle from the one in which I had arrived. When we had taken the decision to move into the mobile home the previous year, one of the first things to go to help towards the bills was my lorry and, as a result, we now had to resort to hiring and borrowing vehicles to get the horses around any great distance. Sadly, prior to the course, a friend had let us down at the last minute and the only way I could get here at such notice was to hire a specialist horse transporter – much to Robert's horror when he found out the cost. Arnie and I had looked very grand arriving on the course, pulling up in a very smart six-berth special when there were only the two of us! It looked like Robert had now taken control of the situation much more to his satisfaction, driving a beaten-up old estate car with a trailer that looked as if it had seen better days.

'Absolute bargain!' he said, noting the look of horror on my face and trying desperately to justify his actions. 'Just £10 for the trailer and £30 for the car, and it's hardly used any petrol!' He looked for my approval as I examined the state of the trailer. 'Anyway, have you had a nice time? You look very pleased with yourself. How's Arnie?' I decided not to make an issue of the trailer as, nonetheless, I was pleased to see him.

I said my goodbyes to Jackie and Emma, and we swapped phone numbers. I promised to keep in touch with developments and we set about loading Arnie.

'He's big, isn't he?' said Robert, trying to deflect my attention away from the nightmare task of levering Arnie into the tiny trailer. Despite his bad reputation, I had never had any trouble loading Arnie into any vehicle before, though I now had serious doubts as to what he would make of this one. He stood on the ramp which seemed to bow under his weight and looked gingerly inside, mentally trying to measure it up for size.

'Come on, my sweet, let's have a go.' As I coaxed him, he lowered his great head and walked straight in, his flanks brushing against the side of the trailer and the central partition.

'Can't we take the partition out?' Robert asked. But we had nowhere to store it and no means of securing it to the side either. Although Arnie was pretty tightly wedged in, he was at least comfortable and as keen as I was to head back home.

We set off at a steady pace and I proceeded to tell Robert all that had happened over the past few days. For the most part he sat in silence with the odd comment here and there, '. . . and they believed what you said; you mean to say, nobody laughed?'

I explained how supportive they had all been, especially Jackie, and what a help that had been to me.

Suddenly the trailer started to veer violently from side to side, all over the road. 'Slow down! Slow down!' I shouted out. 'For God's sake slow down or it will tip over!'

By now we were on the motorway and just managed to pull in slowly to the hard shoulder before disaster struck. Slightly shaken we both got out to see what was going on.

Robert stuck his head through the jockey door of the trailer where I was calming down Arnie. 'The tyre's burst on the rear of the trailer. I'll go and find one of those emergency phones.'

He was gone some time and I cursed the trailer, and us being stuck there. As each juggernaut went past we were rocked from side to side in its wake. You never realise how noisy motorways can be until you are stuck on the side of one.

'I told them to bring a complete set of tyres for the blasted thing,' said Robert on his return. I looked puzzled at his remark and he added, 'If you get underneath the trailer and check the inside walls of the tyres they are all perished. The outside walls are fine but I never bothered to look at what they were like inside. I just took it for granted they were okay when they let us have the trailer.'

I couldn't believe what I was hearing. Why now? Why us? After such a special few days, why us? The people who had hired us the trailer were friends, so we could hardly rant at them. But how dangerous; we could have been killed; Arnie could have been killed. I felt so frustrated.

Eventually a rescue truck appeared and a smiling, oil-covered figure emerged. He examined the trailer and confirmed what Robert had said, 'You were very lucky you know! Could have been much worse.'

Then he added as he proceeded to change the tyres, 'I'm dreadfully sorry, I've picked up two of the wrong tyres by mistake. I'm going to have to go back for the right ones.'

My jaw hit the ground. 'How long will you be?' I asked as calmly as I could muster.

'I'll be as quick as I can; shouldn't be more than an hour, hour and a half, maybe two.'

As he disappeared into the distance, we watched miserably, finishing off the last of our packet of mints.

A journey that had taken us two hours before, now took six and a half to complete and we arrived back home tired and starving hungry.

After I had finished settling Arnie, making sure that he had suffered no ill effects from the trip, I checked over the other horses to see that they were all right. We had arranged for someone to do our evening stable routine for us or we would have been faced with that now, on top of everything else.

'Tea! That's what we need. Tea!' said Robert cheerily.

As I finished the last of the drying-up from supper, he glanced at me. 'I'm really pleased you were able to talk to someone horsey about all of this.' He paused, deep in thought. 'But did you actually learn anything new on the course?'

I didn't quite know whether to laugh or cry.

'One thing's for certain that I learned.'

'What's that then?'

'Just that things will never be the same again.'

I took my tea and retired to bed leaving him muttering to himself.

3

A Resourceful Man

Ah, home sweet home, ours a ramshackle mobile version situated on the edge of a bird conservation area; our horses at Woodmore's Riding School as it was once known, now a livery yard comprising a higgledy-piggledy collection of buildings used as stables, some original, some converted, some falling down. Prime development site apparently, right on the edge of a new housing estate which was springing up prolifically like daffodils in April.

The yard had shopping mall written all over it. This was the proprietor's hope, anyway. He had been kind enough to inform us of this matter when we had first rung him to enquire about vacancies. 'It may well be that we're not here for much longer, you know. There's a development proposal pending on the site, but if you want stabling for a short time, there's no problem. We've got enough room.'

With this in mind we accepted and found ourselves looking for some equally suitable abode. The caravan. For five years it had been used by avid ornithologists as an office and observation post just on the edge of Woodbury Common. With their needs having been very basic and ours currently geared towards our three dogs, we accepted this as our home for what, we hoped, would be a short time.

It was, without doubt, basic. The dogs loved it, running up and down its length without a care in the world, flinging old bones and odd socks wherever they pleased; no smart furniture to worry about, nothing to knock over or spoil. Yippee!

For myself, I kept a very positive outlook. It had a lovely glass conservatory at one end where the morning sun flooded in, rising over the trees, awakening the birds to their dawn chorus. It also let in the pouring rain as the storm clouds, rolling inland from the sea, paused overhead to unload their burden at the highest point. It *also* admitted the fearsome east wind that blew hard, gathering momentum over the sweeping common land surrounding us. Sometimes you could sit quietly, reading a book or writing a letter, and experience all three elements in quick succession.

At such times my positive outlook would seek solace in the living-room; picking my way along the corridor, tripping over dog toys and bones, balancing myself as the buffeting wind rocked the entire structure, pausing to collect any water containers which were now full from the rain leaking through the roof, and emptying and replacing these. In the living-room itself we had all the home comforts one could ever want! Lovely red flocked wallpaper complemented by a most dignified carpet of huge mustard, red and brown swirls, further enhanced by curtains of broad horizontal brown and cream stripes. I even took a photo of the carpet for posterity on one occasion!

Not wishing to sound ungrateful or bemoaning, I reminded myself now, that we were considerably better off than some people. At least we had a roof over our heads, albeit a bit leaky; shelter from the wind, albeit a bit unstable; and a lovely setting within the sprawling common and the woodland.

To accompany this thought, the caravan began to shudder violently with the vibration of a laden quarry lorry rumbling past. Unfortunately, while the west wing of our home rested in the glorious countryside, the east wing nestled alongside a road that provided access for the large lorries to and from the quarry, some braking violently as they gathered speed downhill towards the crossroads, others revving and gear changing as they heaved their laden weight uphill. The drivers, skilled men, knowing their vehicles and the road well, executed their gear changing, double declutching or application of air breaks with consummate ease, right beside our living-room.

Never mind, I wasn't here often during the day and it was quieter in the evenings, weather permitting; and we *were* fortunate to live so close to where owls called to each other in the still of night and foxes barked and screeched, chasing each other over the common. Such fun. Fizz, Robert's working collie, would often fail to contain her excitement at such moments and would leap through a window setting off in pursuit, Robert staggering after her in hastily pulled-on wellies, jumper rumpled around his middle and half-shut eyes. Fun for the dog and the foxes but not such fun for Robert at 1.30 in the morning, while I would feign sleep, sound and solid. Lying snugly warm under the feather duvet, feet pulled up underneath me lest they stretch out and touch the outside wall at the bottom of the bed where the condensation streamed, I would marvel at Robert's speed and agility, trampling and stuttering through the woodland, bellowing at

Fizz and topping it all with a four-fingered whistle fit to launch the *Queen Mary* from her docks. What heaven to live in the countryside – never a dull moment.

The yard itself was much the same. Perched on high ground on the other side of the common about four miles away. A lovely drive of about ten minutes or so, depending upon the number of quarry lorries making their way to and fro.

On this, my first morning back after the course, Robert and I pulled into the yard and parked alongside the other livery owners. The car-park was hard standing, all the cars facing the ever-growing housing estate. Privacy being a priority, their gaze and ours was blocked by Mountainous Muckheaps numbers one and five. Stacked in between them lay numerous and varied piles of wood, ironmongery, tyres, buckets, baths and pallets, affectionately known as 'come-in-handy gear'.

'What a resourceful man,' Robert exclaimed, his eyes lighting up as he surveyed the Aladdin's cave of treasures.

Neville, the owner, was indeed a resourceful man, usually greeting us in the mornings with a big booming 'Morrrn-in!', accompanied by his faithful Alsatian, Bessie, who, in synchronisation, would begin a great volley of ferocious barking. 'QUIET!' would come the bellowed retort and she always was.

As I made my way to the feed room, an old Nissen hut with an asbestos roof, passing Mountainous Muckheap number three on the way, Neville boomed, 'We're using number four muckheap from now on as the others are rotting down nicely – if you would, please.'

'No problem,' I muttered, tripping over six of Neville's rescued chickens who were waiting hopefully in the Nissen hut doorway for feed to be put into buckets. Making breakfast was a nightmare. I had every understanding of, and admired, Neville's compassionate nature and his desire to rescue these ex-battery hens and the bruised and battered older cockerels, but they downed more of the feed than the horses did! As fast as one put scoop from bin to bucket it became submerged under a sea of chickens. Flapping at them and shooing them away did no good; they paused briefly, eyed you sideways and began their onslaught again. It took skill, dexterity and surprise tactics to make up the feeds; firmly shutting the front door in the face of the hens then running the length of the hut to slam the rear door, rushing back to the feed bins, whipping the lids off and flinging feed from bin to bucket with lightning speed, before the barrage of feathered friends arrived again each time the door opened. No measuring and carefully prepared rations here, just a bucket of food and think yourself lucky if it didn't have a chicken in it!

Success! Making my way to the tack room for the honey which I mixed with hot water for some of the horses, I encountered a similar scenario with the wasps. They lived happily somewhere around Monstrous Muckheap number three, right next to the tack room which was a garden shed with a piano stored at one end, just in case one ever felt the need to burst into song. This also sported a leaky roof and, provided one didn't move too quickly, it managed to remain fairly stable on its rotten struts, merely emitting a few creaks and groans to remind you to tread carefully and with respect.

Outside the door, slightly to the right, was a beautiful, big, old oak tree which had been left, to Neville's credit, intact, but concreted in at the base. In the very heart of its boughs, and nearly camouflaged by the foliage, I could just make out what looked like a stereo speaker. Peering at it, I dismissed it as more 'come-in-handy gear'. I was wrong. Sally, Neville's daughter, loved her music and had insisted that her brother, Graham, install a speaker in the tree so that, wherever she might be in the yard, or even when riding her horse on the common, she would not be without music.

As I mixed up the honey for the horses, I put a little aside, as usual, on the upturned lid for the hovering wasps. I personally have no problems with wasps and appreciate that they have a role to fill decreed by nature. They are sensitive little creatures and find their way through their environment by picking up sound and vibration from their immediate surroundings. Sally chose that particular moment to switch on her speaker. Techno music was upon us, and at 1,000 decibels or so it seemed.

The floor shook, creaked and vibrated, the kettle nearly boiled over. Honey jar clasped firmly in my left hand, the spoon resonated in my right as I made a vain attempt to direct it into the jar. As I missed, I glanced at the lid. The wasps hovered and buzzed around the upturned lid in a demented state. They couldn't land or stay still, try as hard as they might; the techno vibes were just too powerful. As the lid jiggled around on the old office table, the wasps swooped on and off, up and down, back and forth, as if caught in the force of a gale. It was all too much for their delicate senses. Some up-ended and landed on their backs in the honey, others buzzed furiously around the ceiling of the shed, startled and distressed, others landed on me, clinging to my jacket for security.

Vibrating to my very core, I turned to look out of the door. There I saw seven horses, two of which were mine, with eyes out on stalks, coats standing on end, ears back, ramrod straight necks shot out over stable doors as if electrocuted. The little Arab to my left found himself sliding into his stable door giving his pasterns and knees a hefty whack.

Neville was as cool as a cucumber, continuing his bawled conversation with Robert, oblivious to the techno intrusion. His dog, Bessie, however, was not so serene. From standing in a healthy upright position beside him she had flung herself to the ground, chin flat on the floor, forepaws outstretched, managing to wedge her head between Neville's rubber-clad legs. Wellies as ear mufflers! Talk about save yourself and never mind the rest of us!

Sally skipped out into the yard greeting everyone with her cheery smile and a blithe 'Hiya!'. At least, I think that's what she said. I couldn't hear her, but I surmised that it was something of that nature from the shape of her mouth and lips.

Some half-hour later she rode her horse out of the yard leaving us all enshrouded in electro-techno. No one had the bottle to suggest to this 16-year-old that her music was, perhaps, not as appealing to the rest of us as it was to her, let alone had the nerve to switch it off and risk the wrath of young hormones in full flurry. I could remember being in a similar position myself and being more than a little offended when presented with a pair of stout headphones on one birthday.

Mucking out Arnie's stable, which was some distance from the tree but, nevertheless, left him cringing and boring his head into his haynet, I contemplated the strong hold that we have over animals. We decide what they should eat, what they should wear, where they should live, and even which type of music they should be subjected to. I personally did not like techno, nor did Arnie, nor Herbie, nor any of my other horses for that matter. But was it just because *I* didn't? Were they responding to my feelings on the matter or was it a genuine choosing on their part?

Examining human/animal relationships, Neville's dog, Bessie, was a case in point, and her behaviour intrigued me. She was a rescue dog and no longer young in years. Without fail she greeted everyone, both in the morning and in the evening, with a barrage of barking, even though we were familiar to her. Quite understandable if one were new, but after weeks, months, and in some instances years, to continue this behaviour seemed without logic.

Bessie was quite obviously devoted to Neville. Despite her aching limbs she would wait patiently outside the house for his return should he leave the yard, only becoming distracted from her vigil by the necessity to bark at any arrival to the premises. Her manner, although not vicious, was threatening. Apart from this she was a truly nice dog, following Neville everywhere and doing exactly as he bade her. She became friendly in his presence and, providing that he was there, was happy to accept biscuits, a tummy rub, or a pat from the rest of us at the yard.

I had watched her with interest and a large element of curiosity on many occasions as she followed Neville from muckheap to muckheap, stable to stable, horse to horse, staring adoringly at the seat of his pants and never breaking off to do doggy things like sniff around the yard or run and play. While her age and stiffness could well have accounted for this, it struck me that there was perhaps more to it than appeared on the surface.

So with my newly gained confidence following the course with Emma, and also out of personal interest, I decided to ask Bessie why she behaved as she did. I would state here categorically that I, like every devoted dog owner, know when my own dogs are unwell, or unhappy, or in need of something. Foxi, one of my dogs, had once transmitted to me whilst I was driving, that she was going to vomit if I did not pull over and let her out of the car. On that occasion, unfortunately, I did not pay any attention, and I learned the hard way. I had never until now, however, considered whether the rapport that I had with horses would fully stretch to other animals as well.

Putting myself to the test, I sought Bessie out in a quiet moment and asked her, in the best way that I could, why she barked so vehemently at everybody even when she knew them well.

Her reply came like a bolt from the blue; a flooding series of images, flashing through my mind in quick succession, one after the other. Initially I felt that I had been too slow to catch them, but I hadn't. It was like flicking through a child's moving image book where each page holds a cartoon or character which, on its own, appears static, but when flicked through at speed with all the other pages, suddenly springs into life to perform a series of movements.

I was astounded and fascinated. The images were so clear and so full of information that it took me a little while to decode them into my own language, the essence of which I can put into words but, even now, still feel that so much more was offered than I was equipped to catch at that time.

She explained a time of great sorrow and desolation, emptiness, with no love in her life, and then the arrival of Neville who was the closest thing to love she had known. Although it was not the purest form of love it was the best that she had been offered. She respected him and loved him but also knew that she was not considered his equal; she had a role to fulfil for him and this she would do.

Part of this role required loyalty, hence the unerring following, staring at what I had perceived to be the seat of his pants, but was in fact, the easiest position for her from which to catch his thoughts. Her senses were not as acute as those of a young, strong dog, and it was much easier for her to pick up Neville's thoughts from behind him, flowing as they did like a vapour trail.

Her barking at every arrival was also part of the deal. Whilst he often bellowed at her to be quiet, he did, in reality, enjoy the fact that she kept people in their place on his behalf. She was not territorial, but he was – very much so. She meant no harm, would not hurt anyone, but felt it necessary to uphold his desires.

When I had deciphered this, it all became glaringly obvious. Some livery owners she barked at with greater vim and vigour than others, yet this was not consistent, and varied depending on who was in, or out, of favour with Neville at the time. I thanked her profusely and asked whether she would mind not barking at me. She lowered her eyes and her head ever so slightly, a reticent 'yes' or perhaps an 'okay'.

She remained true to her word over the next ten days or so without a problem. Her eyesight and sense of smell were not as sharp as they could be, so, often when I first pulled up in the car she would begin with a hefty 'woof' or two, then stop once she had determined my identity. I was delighted, I had had a meaningful conversation with a dog, a remarkable event in its own right, but on top of that, she had made a choice and honoured it. 'Life is amazing,' I thought whenever I saw her.

Over the following days, something else came to my attention and a horrible realisation dawned on me. Neville had noticed the change in behaviour of his faithful dog – and he was not amused.

I felt terrible. I had not entirely realised how important the whole affair was to both Bessie and Neville. She performed his requests with a sense of duty, out of the love that she felt for him. He was special to her and she to him. By my requesting her to change her behaviour, she could not now fully oblige Neville and, therefore, was placed in an impossible predicament. Within Neville's increasingly complicated life: the muckheaps; finances; leaking, creaking fragile structures; barren fields with hungry horses squabbling over loose hay, kicking and biting each other and breaking down fences; growing complaints from owners about missing tools, dangerous paddocks etc., the one thing he could trust and rely on among the mayhem was the unwavering loyalty of his dog. No matter what the day brought, Bessie was ever faithful, keeping things in order and upholding his position among the rest of us.

The value of this to Neville must have been very special. No matter who let him down, or gave him a hard time, his dog never did. Now it must seem as if this, too, was slipping away. When Bessie had shown me her life, I had been too naïve to grasp fully the importance of her role. She understood far more of the Neville behind the façade than any of us people probably ever would. I was obviously honoured and privileged to have been given her information, but I had overlooked the depth and honesty within her.

She had listened to me, had stopped barking, but at what cost? The only benefit was perhaps to myself. Other livery owners were not best pleased that she barked at them and not at me. It gained me no admiration or respect from them, only hostility and sideways glances. Neville was gutted. The one thing in life that he had believed to be safe, was his dog's love. And now, even that was under threat. Worst of all, the dog was unhappy, divided in loyalty and misinterpreted, yet still with a greater understanding than I personally had.

I apologised. I really was very, very sorry. The real gift for me had been the conversation, that special moment when she had opened her heart and explained her life. I had completely overlooked that, and now I was appalled with myself.

'Bessie, bark at me. Bark at me all you like. I'm so sorry. If you need to, bark at me all day long and I'll thank you for it. Whatever it takes to put things right, you must do.'

From that day on she did and I was greeted with the full volley, in fact much more so than before. Neville was appeased, the other owners were no longer suspicious. And myself? I gained a greater respect for the gift that I have.

Thank you, Bessie.

4

A Bit of a Knack

Making sure that all our horses were comfortable with their beds tidied and their individual needs attended to, Robert and I made haste to leave. Time was getting on. It was nearly 12.30 p.m. Quickly scrabbling our tools together, grabbing the last of the sweepings and bundling them into a skip, we sprinted to the Nissen hut. Whooshing the ever-hopeful chickens aside, we made lunch for the horses in double quick time. Countdown was on! Alarm bells were ringing!

'I don't think we're going to make it, you know, Robert. We're scuppered.'

He glanced at his watch and frowned. 'Get a move on! We might be lucky.'

Grabbing four buckets in one swift movement, flinging them under his arm, he shot out of the hut and made a dash for the top yard. Following his lead, I grabbed the remaining three buckets and sprinted down to our horses residing in the bottom yard.

Bolting their doors as quickly as possible I met Robert in the alley leading back to the Nissen hut, both of us travelling so fast we nearly collided. Buckets launched from the hut doorway landed neatly in their place beside the feed bins. Outside door slammed shut and bolted, we glanced at each other. Maybe! We might just have made it!

Setting off once more at a gallop towards the carpark, past Mountainous Muckheap number three and the tack room, avoiding Neville's lorry, from which tumbling bales of straw and hay were bouncing off the lowered ramp, we skipped over water-filled potholes, sighted Mountainous Muckheap number five, and, thinking we had made it, were brought to a most abrupt halt.

'Ello Neveelle!' The shrill Midlands accent split the air.

'Ello Robert! Ello Nicci! Alroight? Oooh! 'Ave I 'ad a mornin' of eet! I've brought Malcolm's sandwiches an' 'is coffee. Is 'e not 'ere yet? Ello-ar-Eddie!' This last directed towards the stable of a pony and delivered as one word. Amy continued, fascinatingly without seeming to draw breath.

'Ahh, I loove 'eem t' bits y'know. 'E always calls t' me y'know. I didn't used t'like 'eem when 'e were younger but I loove 'eem to bits now! Are y'alroight ar Neveelle? I saw Rosie this mornin' in the surgery – is she alroight? 'Ang on ar Eddie, I'm just comin'! Ooooh look, 'ere's ar Malcolm. Malcolm!' Her tone reached fever pitch.

'The man from the Gas Board came this mornin' – 'e's on about ar meter but I told 'eem, "That's not roight" – I sent 'eem packin', I did. I'm goin' to ring them this afternoon and give them what for, y'know – that's twice they've done that to us now, y'know – I told 'eem straight, I'm 'avin' none of eet!' she confided to the rest of us.

'Alroight ar Eddie, I'm comin'! Ooooh! Look at the time, I've got to get back and get me nets in to soak. Come on ar Malcolm, it's twenty-five to one! I've got your sandwiches 'ere. 'Urry oop! 'Urry oop!'

Malcolm had not yet managed to get out of the car. He had barely switched off the ignition and undone his seat-belt, but make no mistake he could hear Amy. Everybody could. That was the thing about Woodmore's, everyone was loud. Eddie the pony neighed back his equally raucous greeting and Neville stopped in his chore of unloading the hay.

'Allo darlin'! 'Ow are you, me love?' he boomed over and above the shrill deluge of Amy's gabbled facts and complaints.

Robert and I were now trapped in the middle of them. Both parties advanced on each other talking at the same time, one becoming more shrill, the other bellowing, bestowing upon each other a cascade of words, neither one listening to the other. No need for Robert or myself to reply, really, they would not have noticed, being far too embroiled in their verbal jousting match.

Malcolm brought up the rear. 'Alroight. Alroight.' Uttered not as a question like Amy, but as the statement of a man resigned. 'Language is a strange thing,' was my passing thought.

These were the 'Diddy People', known as such to Robert and myself due to their lack of height. I myself am not particularly tall but I way overshadowed both Amy and Malcolm, which probably accounted for the fact that they owned a 12.2hh Welsh Mountain pony, namely Eddie, or 'Ar Eddie' as he was affectionately known.

Luckily, Neville was in fine humour this particular day and was only too delighted to uphold the courtesy of roaring back in response to Amy's exhausting delivery. Malcolm, running from hay shed to water tap, was fulfilling 'Ar Eddie's' most urgent needs, while Amy waved a cellophane-wrapped, giant, Black Country sandwich in his general direction, like a tantalising reward for his labours.

As Malcolm rushed back and forward, still muttering, 'Alroight. Alroight. Don't rush me. I'm goin' as fast as I can, alroight,' Amy had not paused in her conversation with Neville, nor he with her. They both appeared to draw strength from each other, becoming more embroiled in the debate of the day.

Robert and I both knew that this would continue for the next hour throughout Malcolm's hard-earned lunch break as it did every weekday. Robert eyed the sandwich still being wafted about with no apparent claim of ownership. 'That looks good,' he mouthed at me, very tempted to claim it for himself. I restrained him and we shuffled sideways towards the car. All was usually well if one stood still and listened, but woe betide you if you were spotted trying to sidle away!

Today fate was on our side and, creeping crablike towards the muckheap and our car, we managed our getaway. Once our hands were firmly on the door handles, we raised our arms, cheerily waved 'Bye,' and diving into the car, prayed she would start. She was, it had to be said, a little temperamental and, although had never actually failed us, she had on certain occasions given us serious doubts as to whether she ought to go to the great scrap heap in the sky. Today she fired up well, the engine undoubtedly having drawn heat from Mountainous Muckheap number five, and we were away, chugging along the pitted drive towards the common and home.

Back at the caravan I settled myself in front of the fire in the living-room with my customary cup of tea and cigarette.

Robert hurried back from the end bedroom, which we disguised as an office, where he had been checking the answerphone messages. He could hardly contain his excitement.

'The *Sunday Express*!' he cried, pointing to the living-room extension, jumping up and down with glee. 'They want to interview you!'

Choking on my tea I looked at Robert to see if he was serious. Apparently so! My mind was now racing ten to the dozen as Robert leapt about excitedly. He stammered that according to the answerphone message Juliette, the reporter, would be calling back very shortly.

'What are you going to say?' he asked nervously.

'I don't know yet. I'll just answer whatever she asks, I suppose. I'm sure inspiration will come from somewhere.'

I was surprised, disbelieving, excited and yet calm, seemingly all at once. My mind churned. 'Why does she want to talk to me? How wonderful. Oh God, I hope she doesn't intend to pull me to pieces.

No, if that were the case, she wouldn't have rung – surely.' There it was
. . . the phone had begun to ring.

I picked up the receiver with every intention of sounding business-
like and professional, as if this sort of thing occurred all the time. I
stated our number with perfect enunciation and clarity, my apparent
composure surprising me since my heart was pounding in my mouth.

I heard a lovely, friendly voice coming through the receiver. Juliette.
She explained who she was, why she was telephoning, and her
intention to write a piece for her newspaper. She appeared very fair
and honest, explaining that her connection had come through her
mother. She had met someone at a dinner party who had attended
Emma's riding course with me. Over dinner, apparently, I had been the
topic of excited conversation. Juliette had found the subject matter
genuinely fascinating when relayed to her, believing that it would
make an interesting article.

We talked at great length. Juliette wanted to know my full life
history, but particularly when, and how, I had first become aware of
my gift. I experienced a feeling of great shyness and reticence. In spite
of my 'coming out of the closet' on the riding course, I still found it
difficult to explain myself to others, especially strangers, and
especially after so many years of protective silence for fear of being
misunderstood, or worse, branded a nutcase.

But thanks to Juliette's skilled and sympathetic probing, I found
myself chatting with ease, telling her that my earliest memory was of
being taken to the stables by my mother at the age of two or three, and
being allowed to sit on the cavalry horses. My father was an army
doctor, then stationed in Germany, and my mother used to ride at the
Saddle Club, often taking my brother and myself as a treat.

My father's next posting was in Cyprus and the whole family drove
there across Europe staying in hotels and lodges overnight. By this
time I was five years old and it became our custom to collect the sugar
cubes from the breakfast tables in order to feed them to any horses or
ponies we encountered on the day's journey. I know that children
everywhere like to do this, but for me it was much more than just the
pleasure of feeding treats to the occasional horse. I was compelled to
stop for every horse, pony or donkey that I saw, and I mean *compelled*.
It was imperative to me and I would order my father to stop with an
urgency that I did not, at that age, understand.

My parents, for their part, were incredibly understanding, waiting
patiently in the car as I presented the sugar to the animals, many of
them broken down by years of poor nourishment, overwork,

untreated sores, badly fitting tack and shoes etc. I would make sure that they got their sugar, even placing it in the mouths of those too wearied or brain deadened to notice that I was there, and that I cared. It was so important to me that they recognise that someone did, and I would lift the blinkers of the saddest cases, looking into their eyes and saying, 'Look. I've brought you something. Something for *you*.'

On one occasion we broke our journey to spend a week in a beautiful villa in the middle of a vineyard. This villa was luxurious in the extreme with stunning views, acres of grounds to play in, and a swimming-pool. It also had a donkey, used for carrying tools and other things for the handyman. I spent the entire week sitting with, talking to, and grooming the donkey, shunning the delights that the villa offered. The handyman was quick to point out the danger of trying to ride the donkey; she would not tolerate anyone on her back. Yet by the end of the week she was letting me sit on her and ride her round on the end of her tether.

Settled in Cyprus, my mother enrolled me in the Saddle Club and I began to have lessons. But there was a complication. Every Saturday that I spent there ended in my crying floods of distraught tears. One day I was put on a 35-year-old, arthritic little pony whose wish to escape was so overwhelming that I clung to the saddle, crying, 'She's going to run away! She wants to gallop off!' The instructor conveyed that she really didn't feel that this particular pony was quite up to that sort of behaviour. Eventually, she suggested to my mother that I didn't need to ride if I really didn't want to.

My father, particularly, was distressed by what he perceived to be my fear but, nevertheless, I was adamant that I must continue to go. I felt that I *had* to go. I was ashamed and embarrassed by my behaviour and confused by my emotions, unable to explain to my parents or to myself how I felt. Every Saturday brought with it a feeling of dread. I found the whole business of going to the stables both traumatic and confusing. Then, one day, a very nice instructor gave me a lesson on the lunge line on one of the big horses. The lesson lasted just half an hour and sitting there, without reins or stirrups, I felt happy. At the end of the lesson she turned to my mother and said, 'She's going to be really good, you know'.

From that moment on, I knew I was right to keep riding, and my parents' fears were put to rest. Much, much later, I understood that my distress must have been picked up from the ponies I had been riding, many of which had suffered years of exhaustive work in carts, or as beasts of burden, before being rescued by the army.

When I was about 11 my father was posted back to Germany. My parents continued to encourage me through the Pony Club, and bought me my first pony. This particular pony came to me by default. His name was Tutenkhamun, or Toots as he became known. He was sold because he had become unridable and no one else would buy him, his reputation having spread far and wide. He would buck, quite literally, like a bronco, a series of bone-shaking handstands with his head jammed firmly between his knees and his body almost vertical. But I fell in love and after a little persuasion he was mine. But I could not stay on board! Time and again I would sail through the air to land in a crumpled heap some yards from my little ejector seat on legs.

My parents, quite naturally, began to mutter about the danger, and I feared for his future. My frustration was paramount. Then, one particular day, as he began his usual cabaret act, I leaned hard back, feeling his bottom bashing the back of my head. Waiting for the by now familiar feeling of flying, accompanied by the inevitable crash landing, it never came. I had done it. 'Don't you *ever* do that to me again!' I said, from the bottom of my boots. From that moment on, he never bucked again, and I earned myself considerable kudos as we proceeded our way through the usual Pony Club activities.

Toots was eventually, sadly outgrown, being followed by another pony, Tam O'Shanter, and he, in turn, was retired and replaced by Fantino. Tino was an Arab, 14.2hh, and I kept him at the yard of an international German showjumper. This chap had a yard full of great, gleaming, Hanoverian horseflesh, and my little Arab was definitely out of place, dismissed by the great man as 'a ponny'. Nevertheless, he was kind enough to take us on and give us lessons, although there were no concessions to be made for 'the ponny'.

'If you want to learn to jump, he must learn to jump like a horse.' And learn we did, benefiting from his instruction so well that we won a large cup, beating many of his own horses over a daunting course. I felt that we had struck a great blow for 'ponnykind'.

Once again my father was posted, this time back to England, where I found myself reluctantly in the middle of my 'A' levels. Desperately wanting to work with horses, I was thwarted by career officer and parental pressure. But help came from an unlikely source. One of the books set for my English Literature course was Franz Kafka's *Metamorphosis*, a bleak and distressing tale of a man who turns into a beetle. I couldn't cope. That was it. I managed to wangle my way onto a Youth Training Scheme at a small yard with hunters and a couple of point-to-pointers. My career in the world of racing had begun.

From then on I was to grow increasingly aware that I was different. At the age of 17 I was not yet astute enough to realise that others did not share the same understanding of horses as myself. Nor did they appreciate my attempts to educate them, or put the record straight on behalf of the horse. I found myself saying things or doing things that earned me derision and contempt from experienced and renowned professionals. I was labelled dreamy, lazy, sentimental and cocky in turn.

Juliette was sympathetic and understanding as I explained all this to her and I warmed towards her. It was much easier to talk to her than I would have ever thought possible.

I continued to tell my story. Juliette was keen to hear more about my time spent in racing. I explained how, during a stint as a lass in the yard of a well-known Flat racing trainer, I quickly learned to keep my mouth shut. I was, by now, experiencing all manner of pains and emotions on a daily basis and it was beginning to dawn on me that these were coming from the horses. I would ride a particular horse and be petrified to leave the yard, another and I would turn into an aggressive thug, jostling the other horses and riders for position. Others I would dismount from and almost collapse from the pain in my knees and ankles; sometimes my sinuses would feel close to exploding, or my eyes would itch and stream. And on it went.

From there I moved to a small mixed yard of Flat and National Hunt horses. That was fun. We were a friendly team without the pressures of the smarter, glossier yards and we muddled through our training programmes in a somewhat haphazard fashion. But the atmosphere was good and I was getting to ride a lot, and over fences too. I was also starting to earn respect for what I was able to achieve with the horses, mainly by being able to stay on board the difficult ones and the 'loonies'.

On one occasion I was working the yard's prized possession on the gallops, dawdling along at an easy lope. As we finished and I pulled up alongside Jim, the trainer, he asked me, 'What happened there?'

Blithely I replied, speaking for the horse, 'He didn't want to go.'

'Didn't bloody want to!? You're not supposed to ask them, you're supposed to bloody tell them!' he roared at me.

Put firmly in my place I decided to maintain my silence with regard to my gift for fear of further ridicule, merely allowing the others to believe that I had 'a bit of a knack'.

By now I was well and truly bitten by the racing bug and wanted to race myself. Conditional National Hunt jockeys' licences (equivalent to Apprentice on the Flat) are fiercely competed for, and so I grabbed the opportunity offered by a yard in Jersey. There I was able to achieve my ambition. I raced four times once over hurdles and three times on the flat, managing to achieve a fourth and second placing.

Eventually I was able to return to England to continue my racing in a mixed yard where I was truly in my element. For the first time I was allowed free rein. Not only was I racing but I was also responsible for assessing horses, deciding what each horse was best at in terms of distance and ability; allocating horses to those lads and lasses I felt would get the best out of them; deciding which horses would complement each other in training, in terms of giving confidence or support to one another; and also deciding the best alternative career for any which were obviously not going to make the grade as racehorses. Some of this was learned, but mostly I just knew what to do.

Unfortunately, there was still a divide between myself and the other staff. I would make myself unpopular by partnering someone with a less than favourite steed, then be unable to explain the decision to their satisfaction. I would admonish others for whacking or shouting at any of the horses, then be found guilty of doing the same myself. There was no way that I could make them understand that when I did it my intent was different from theirs and that, in horse parlance, it made perfect sense.

By now I yearned to run my own yard. Taking the plunge, I replied to an advert in *Horse and Hound* for a tenant for a small yard on a farm in Somerset. I was interviewed by the farm manager. 'What an arrogant man!' I found myself thinking, as he grilled me to assess my suitability. That arrogant man was Robert, and 18 months later, I married him!

Juliette and I paused in our conversation to laugh at this. 'So do you still think he's arrogant?' she asked.

'Only when he doesn't make the tea fast enough,' I replied, miming at Robert for another cup and grinning at his feigned look of wounded pride.

I had thoroughly enjoyed talking to Juliette and any concerns I had had about the honesty and integrity of journalists had been laid to rest. She asked me for some instances of communication with specific horses for her to include in the interview. I outlined a few cases and then Douggie sprang to mind.

'He was a large thoroughbred racehorse,' I explained. 'Not so much tall as big boned. A typical, old-fashioned, Irish 'chaser type. He was in training, at the time when I met him, with a very good, local National Hunt trainer who was young and up-and-coming.

'I was freelancing and, in between looking after the two liveries I had in my yard, I would clean an old people's home, do odd jobs on the farm for Robert – who believed wholeheartedly in the system of barter and delighted in doing deals for bales of hay, something to do with his Scottish heritage, no doubt – and, in addition to all this, also blunder my way through a gardening job.'

Juliette laughed. 'What on earth possessed you to do all that?'

'Well, it was a necessity really, to make ends meet and to keep the yard going with some distant notion of the future. But I did spend most of my time yearning to ride racehorses again, which was why I was so delighted to be riding out for the aforementioned trainer, despite the fact that this job was unpaid.'

'Tell me about Douggie,' begged Juliette.

'How much time do you have? Once I start reminiscing, I could talk you to sleep.'

'Go on, this is fascinating.'

My mind swam back to a lovely sunny morning in early April. I had pulled into the trainer's yard at about 9.15 a.m. while all the other lads and lasses were in having breakfast. The procedure for them was to arrive at 7 o'clock, muck out their three horses and then ride out one lot. The trainer made the decision the night before on who would ride what, and where they would go to do the work. All the rides were carefully planned to determine the quality of fittening work the horses were to achieve.

This information was then pinned on *The Board*.

Quite a ritual, really. Every morning, 12 stable staff clustered round a board on the wall either shrieking and laughing, groaning, or muttering stuff such as 'I must have done something to upset him. He's obviously got it in for me today'; some incensed that their favourite ride had been allocated to somebody else. This, perhaps, caused the greatest consternation with rude words and insults often being flung at the offending party. 'You couldn't sit up straight in bed, let alone ride that horse.' Another favourite being, 'You couldn't ride one side of that horse.' Such colloquialisms had vitriolic depth of meaning that would turn your grandmother in her grave, and yet to those outside the racing fraternity they would probably bring a quizzical furrow to the brow: 'What on earth can they mean?'

I was respectful of these necessary rituals and, although I enjoyed them, was still very aware that I might be intruding upon someone else's beloved horse, and that my generous offer to ride out might not be appreciated by them. Still, I was prepared to take the flak for the pleasure of the ride.

On this particular morning, the information on *The Board* brought huge hilarity and ample opportunity for targeting victims of the trainer's warped sense of humour.

'Beach Ride' was the delegation. Enough to set them all off, particularly those lads whose sharp wit would have earned them standing ovations as comedians.

Scanning down the list, I saw my name alongside that of Douggie and, even though I knew nothing about the horse, I quickly realised that I was today's victim. I felt all eyes were on me, although, I confess, I was not alone. Alison had been similarly targeted.

Those who were in the clear joined in with jokes, quips, and cleverly contrived songs, throughout which the common theme was sou'westers, waterproofs, bath time, and waterings, etc.

I stood quite still, uncertainly trying to ascertain the truth. Were they joking or did they mean it?

Alison had no such hesitation. 'Sod this!' she muttered, reaching for her waterproofs with a determined air and ramming her right leg into her yellow trousers, hopping around the tack room, various obscenities issuing from her lips. This, of course, brought more amusement from the others, some of whom were clutching their sides silently, having passed through mirth into paralysis.

I looked at Mark, the head lad, naïvely thinking that he would tell me the truth.

'Are you winding me up or do you mean it?'

This brought a volley of different answers simultaneously from the assembled crowd.

'Yeah, he loves the beach.'

'No, he's a brute. He'll drop you in the drink for a pastime.'

I realised there was little point in asking. I might just as well wait and see. Requesting directions for Douggie's stable, I collected my tack from the car. 'I haven't brought my waterproofs, anyway,' I thought.

Threading my way through the rambling yard, I found Douggie, renowned for his lovely, smiley, bay face, big white blaze, big brown eyes, perfectly formed, pricked ears, and big chomping teeth. This information had been volunteered by the girl who looked after him as I'd passed her briefly in the yard. She obviously was not mortally wounded by the fact that I was to ride him, and, moreover, was very helpful, warning me, 'Watch your bosoms. He took a bloody great chunk out of mine the other day.'

I wasn't sure what to say, but I thought that 'thank you' would do nicely. I tacked him up, watching my bosoms carefully. All went well. We all clattered out into the yard, vaulted on from a low brick wall, and headed off in a long string towards the beach, Alison sticking out like a sore thumb, decked as she was in heavy duty rain gear on such a lovely, sunny day.

Riding Douggie, his personality began to become apparent to me. He was lovely to sit on, big and broad and comfortable, but his demeanour was profound. He stomped up the road, those lovely big shoulders taking short, pounding steps on the tarmac, that lovely round bottom clamped underneath him, hind feet paddling away, his beautiful neck scrunched up like a concertina, those ears, so beautifully shaped now twisted backwards, firmly jammed against the sides of his head. Although I couldn't see, I also knew that his nostrils were wrinkled, his teeth were gritted and he was backing off the bit. Well, at least my bosoms were out of reach.

We were trotting now, Douggie stomping uphill, more and more like a concertina, Alison cursing that her waterproofs were causing a dramatic rise in her body temperature, other lads and lasses gossiping, extolling the virtues of one jockey or another or discussing the next day's runners, someone fine-tuning the lyrics and melody of the 'Beach Ride Song'.

As we settled back to a walk, I suddenly found myself saying to Douggie, 'Don't think like that.' Not by way of a reprimand, nor as an order, simply, 'Don't think like that.'

The effect upon him was profound. He faltered in his stompy gait for a split second, then pricked his ears and began to relax. His shoulders dropped and his stride lengthened, his quarters began to soften and swing, his tail lifted and his gait became more flowing, his neck began to reach out and he accepted the bit, starting to play with it in his mouth. Whilst sitting quietly on him, I had caught his deepest thoughts, in an unconscious way, and he had heard my reply and responded.

He was afraid. Afraid of the water. The coldness of it and also the bigness of it. The way it came rushing at him, pulling at his legs, up under his belly and around his groin. Afraid of the disorientation, of the mass of movement, and of not being able to see the bottom, only the swirling mass of cold, angry force. He knew it was alive, a living, frothing, powerful form of life, dark and cold and without thought or feeling, and it put the fear of God into him.

We arrived at the beach. The horses filed into the water one after the other, some jogging, some splashing, some with reluctance, others with delight. I positioned Douggie close up behind the horse in front so that he could focus his eyeline on the top of its tail. He liked this idea but, at the last minute, baulked at going in, the tension seizing his body again. He lifted his head and pricked his ears towards the horizon. I could feel his heart pounding. Firmly I took a hold on the reins, gave him a pat and said, 'You'll be all right. Go on in.'

With a little kick, he went bravely forwards to face his terror, into the sea.

We completed two lengths of the beach in the deep water, stones and pebbles on the bottom crunching and slipping away from under his feet, chest high in the strong waves, breasting the current and strong tide in order to make the most of the drag, and all in the name of fitness.

I helped Douggie by keeping my eyeline firmly fixed on the stillest point ahead of me so that he could follow my gaze and keep his balance, stopping his mind from wandering. It demanded a huge amount of self-control on my part and his, and I will always cherish the memory of his bravery and his faith in trusting me, especially when the focal point I was using was the middle of Alison's shining, yellow-waterproofed spine.

We had only another half-length of the shore to complete when disaster struck. My focal point suddenly disappeared! Where once had been yellow waterproofs and a bay horse, was now a blue waistcoat and a chestnut. Alison and her horse had disappeared, spirited away by the demons of the sea.

Suddenly they both reappeared, welling up from beneath the surface, thrashing like fish caught in a net. The bay horse, ears full of water, legs whirling trying to gain a foothold, splashing and choking, spewing water from nose and mouth, appeared, bedecked with Alison, yellow and shiny, upside down, arriving at the surface wellies first followed by elbows and torso, gargling her usual obscenities, somewhat choked by the sea.

In the same instant, Douggie froze. I sat very still and took a big breath downwards as the cascade of water hit us and the swell caused by the frantic splashing slapped way past his belly-line and over his flanks and neck.

'Be still,' I whispered, again not as a command but as a thought, and with purpose. 'Be still.' His heartbeat softened and his body relaxed. He stood like a rock.

Alison and her horse were now both the right way up, dripping and bedraggled with sea water, while the air around them filled with the glorious, chart-topping 'Beach Ride Song', the lyrics of which had obviously spontaneously permeated the minds of the other riders. Everyone joined in with full voice in honour of Alison and her mount, except for myself and Douggie, who throughout all of this had managed to remain as stable and as calm as was possible under the circumstances.

The trainer, meanwhile, who had been observing from the safety of the pebbled beach, having driven down in his car, was wiping tears of mirth from his eyes. In a vain attempt to restore order, he called us over in a semi-broken voice, trying to regain his authority.

We all filed out of the sea and walked past him one by one, dutifully stopping for a brief exchange of words with him in traditional racing style.

'How was he this morning? No coughing?'

'Just the one, Guv, when we first pulled out. After that he was fine.'

Still with tears in his eyes and a croak in his voice, the trainer followed this procedure down the string.

Knowing the importance of this procedure, the importance of the information passed from staff to trainer, and on to owner, I was alarmed at how best to answer. I had not been paying the slightest attention to the assessment of Douggie's fitness, nor his breathing capacity, nor his potential state of readiness to move on in his work. 'Oh, crikey,' I said to Douggie under my breath, 'I'll just have to make it up or something.'

Alison squelched past in front of me, woefully leading her horse and dragging her water-filled wellies up the pebbles. The trainer opened his mouth as if to ask his usual question but, strangely enough, one of the lyrics of the 'Beach Ride Song' sailed past his lips instead, and he doubled over, clutching his middle as Alison trudged past, exercising her repertoire of curses.

Then it was my turn. The trainer had composed himself enough to speak again, although I knew that he would be hooting with laughter all the way back to the yard. I halted Douggie alongside him and waited.

'How did you manage that?' he asked. 'We've never been able to get him in!'

Since every valuable member of staff in racing must always have something to tell the trainer, I said, 'Oh!', patted Douggie and then, looking at the trainer, but still speaking to the horse, said, 'He's all right really.'

Douggie looked at the trainer. His gaze locked briefly, eye to eye with this man. As far as I was concerned, this was Douggie's moment of glory. What he had managed to achieve in terms of self-control, bravery and trust must not be taken from him. I glanced over my shoulder as Douggie and I chose to trot away and met the trainer's searching, bemused glance. Feeling it was impolite not to reply to his implied question in some sort of way, but not knowing how, I merely shrugged my shoulders and allowed Douggie to catch up with his friends.

There was simply too much to explain, and I didn't feel, at the time, that I could have put into words exactly what had happened. Even if I had, I'm not sure that he would have understood. But Douggie did, and I knew that, from that moment on, my bosoms would be safe.

5

The Big Breakfast

I spoke to Juliette several times after our first conversation and we became friends. She wrote a beautiful piece for which I was very grateful.

After the publication of the article, a tidal wave of enquiries followed; people ringing for help, ringing to talk, curious people, and those keen to test my validity. We were surprised and delighted with the response.

One call brought further excitement. The producer of Channel 4's morning show, *The Big Breakfast*, rang in person, asking me if I would appear on the programme if they supplied the horses. In a fit of inspiration, and on an absolute high that I was not alone in caring what horses thought and felt, I said, 'I'll do it.'

And so I did.

Driving up to London on the Sunday evening prior to the next day's show, I arrived and found myself installed in a beautiful plush hotel. I was instructed that a car would collect me at 6 a.m. the following morning and take me to the studio, a real house, for 6.30 where the horses would be waiting for me. The programme would begin at 7 a.m. and I was due on 20 minutes later, after having been given half an hour in which to meet and talk to the horses. I would then be filmed live for three minutes or so, based on my findings.

'Yep,' I had said on the phone, 'no trouble at all. I can do that.' Not a trace of nerves or doubt. Throw caution to the wind and go for it, I'd thought. My nerves and worries must have been on holiday at the time, but they were not going to allow me to do this without them now, and had returned with a vengeance.

Safely settled in my hotel room, I surveyed the selection of delicacies at my disposal in the drinks cabinet and on the menu. Under normal circumstances these would have been a delight but, right now, my nervousness saw to it that I was not to enjoy them.

Battling with both my inner and conscious thoughts, I spent the best part of the evening having a mental argument with myself. 'I should get an early night – no, I should stay awake in case I oversleep. I should go and get something to eat – no, I'll look a fool eating on my own, people will stare and someone will ask me what I'm doing here and they'll never believe I'm on *The Big Breakfast*, and they'll charge me for my meal. I need a cigarette – no, it's a no smoking hotel and, anyway, it's good for me not to smoke.'

In the end, I compromised and had a cigarette behind the curtain. Feeling guilty in case the maids should find out, I watched the pleasure boats go up the Thames.

Who says smoking is no good for you? That night I found peace and solace behind the curtain, and my mind wandered, jogged to a distant memory by the smell of the cigarette smoke.

You see, it's very difficult to explain to people how horses communicate and think. They have enormous understanding, an intelligence that is so easily overlooked or misinterpreted. Their honesty is profound and yet, so often, gets them into trouble.

The cigarette smoke took me back in my mind to Munch who was a very dear friend of mine. In spite of his many physical problems and pain, he maintained a sense of humour and pleasure in life, and was, unlike a few other horses, very understanding of my smoking habit.

Originally, he was brought to my yard for three weeks to do some road work following extensive treatment on his tendons and a year of rest. Those three weeks ended up stretching to two years. I was not the only one who fell madly in love with him. Prior to this he had been in training and had always been a firm favourite, mainly for his sense of humour. While he made all of us laugh with his antics, there was something more about him for me, something much more profound, and this was his intelligence!

He had been in training with me for some time when it became necessary, because of Jockey Club rules, to take him hunting, so that he could qualify to race in point-to-points and hunter 'chases. This would be his first time out with hounds. For this very strong horse and having no brakes thanks to a previously broken jaw, I felt that the hunting field might prove to be more than a little exhilarating!

The meet was very local to us and so I arrived in plenty of time for him to see everything and understand what was going on. As a horse whisperer, I had no intentions of explaining things to him, knowing that he was better off learning from the other horses. Munch was very aware of occasion and was a little uptight on the way to the meet, but was more than happy to look around and relax when we got there.

The trays of drinks offered as a stirrup-cup were fascinating to him. It was customary for everyone to take a glass – and so he did! Not as delicately, perhaps, as he might have done, but, nevertheless, he helped himself, followed by sausage rolls and ham sandwiches which he was not so keen on. After rolling them around in his mouth for a while, he decided that they were not for him and carefully spat them back onto the tray, turning his attention to more alcohol.

To the normal hunting fraternity this would have been considered the height of bad manners, but to me, and luckily those holding the trays, because it was Munch, it was acceptable.

The trays were full of offerings and indeed they were being offered. Everyone was taking something from the trays and expressing their pleasure. For us it was polite to do so, to have declined would have been considered rude and may even have caused offence. It took Munch no more than a moment or two to realise, grasp, and fully understand what was going on and, moreover, to take part in the ritual. Indeed, it filled him with sheer delight to be allowed to do so.

I was sitting on him, marvelling at his powers of comprehension, when the urge for a cigarette hit me. Looping the reins over one arm, not that they were much use anyway thanks to his jaw, I carefully balanced my glass of plum wine in one hand and began the complicated procedure of rolling a cigarette. I had just succeeded in returning my tobacco to my pocket and was inhaling gratefully, when Edward, a foot follower, walked over to say hello.

It was very apparent to me that he was wary of Munch. Whilst Munch had a very beautiful face, he could also do a marvellous impersonation of a Rik Mayall leer, the full benefit of which he bestowed upon Edward now. Standing at a safe distance, Edward eyed Munch's jaws, liberally decked with saliva, sausage roll and ham sandwich. He began to chat politely, unable to hide his obvious look of disdain at Munch's appalling manners, in spite of attempts to mask his thoughts with a smile.

I joined in the polite chit-chat, wine in one hand, cigarette in the other, reins still casually looped over one arm, wondering vaguely why we were engaging in inconsequential banter when Edward was so obviously becoming increasingly horrified. 'What on earth is the matter with the man?' I muttered, more or less to Munch.

Matters came to a dramatic head when Edward said, suddenly, in the middle of discussing the weather, 'Don't fall off, will you?'

'No,' I replied simply, 'I won't,' while in the same instant my unspoken thought was, 'Whatever does he mean by that?'

This thought was without doubt a question that needed a reply. The spoken words were nothing by comparison and it took a horse to point this out to me. Having just marvelled at Munch's powers of perception and understanding, he proceeded to demonstrate them to me in full.

With a squeal, he launched himself onto a grass bank beside the drive, bucked and leaped back onto the gravel, at which point I no longer had a saddle under my bottom, or a horse for that matter.

I was catapulted in a double somersault over his head towards the ground in front of him. As is so often the case on these occasions, time slowed down and I was very aware of my thoughts as I parted company with Munch: 'Wow, the intelligence and honesty of this horse,' 'Eek, my cigarette,' and 'Boy, that ground looks painful,' all in quick succession.

But before I actually hit the drive, Munch lifted his head and jerked his neck back in one swift movement. The reins, which were now looped around my midriff, acted as a brake and I was gently deposited on my bottom with no more force than sitting in a chair, cigarette still clasped between the fingers of my left hand, glass still intact, albeit empty, in my right, and my skull cap between my knees. Thank heavens for Munch's broken jaw.

He looked down at me and I caught his thoughts: 'That's what he meant,' 'Are you all right?' and, 'I thought you said you wouldn't fall off.'

He had taught me a valuable lesson. Not only had he answered my unspoken question, but I realised, in that instant, just how important it is to be honest and speak the truth. Had Edward expressed what he was really thinking, namely that he thought Munch looked dangerous and explosive, I would not have been puzzled by his warning not to fall off. Hence no need for me to wonder what he had meant by his remark, and hence no need for me to be sitting on a gravel drive at this moment.

Time and again I would encounter this incredible truth and honesty among animals and the confusion experienced by them when we, as people, say one thing and mean another. We all know that there is little point in pretending not to fear an animal when, in fact, we do. We recognise that they will always sense our fear. But what about those times when we call a disobedient dog back to us with loving words when, really, we're dying to swipe at it for its insolence in not obeying us. And then we wonder why it still refuses to come. Or those occasions when we're covering up our dread of entering the ring, the fences look enormous, so our horse obliges our uncertainty by refusing three times at the first fence only to be branded a stubborn brute for looking after us. Food for thought, perhaps.

As for Munch, every time thereafter when we went hunting, if I asked him to wait while I rolled myself a cigarette, he would. If I asked him to open and close a gate while the rest of the field galloped through, he would. If I said, 'Munch, I need to pee, let's find somewhere quiet,' he would leave the others, traipse into the undergrowth and wait patiently until I had finished, positioning himself by a log or bank so that I could remount afterwards. Providing one asked with honesty and truth, he was faultless in his generosity. But woe betide those who didn't.

My cigarette had gone out, bringing me back to the present moment: behind the curtain in a plush hotel, trying not to think about the following morning which was looming ever closer.

Feeling more relaxed, I braved the dining-room and, yes, some people did stare, wondering what I was doing there on my own, but the food was delicious. Becoming paranoid about not hearing my alarm call, I stayed awake all night watching movies on Sky TV. I shunned the mini bar preferring to keep my head clear but I did get brave enough to come out from behind the curtain and smoke on the bed.

I must have fallen asleep. The alarm call woke me. Surprise, surprise, not only did it wake me but I sprang from prostrate to upright in 0.2 of a second. I wasn't rude to the man on the end of the shrilling phone who informed me of the time, nor did I crawl back to bed as is so often my wont. Dressing hurriedly, I stuffed my nerves and doubts very firmly into my socks and asked them to stay there. Grabbing my jacket, I went downstairs to meet the car.

When I arrived at *The Big Breakfast*'s house-cum-studio by the canal, two horse trailers were already parked. I could hear one horse neighing loudly and was very tempted to go over, but I was firmly ushered into the studio in the wake of one half of Robson and Jerome, the singing duo, another chap who looked vaguely familiar, and a very pretty girl who was obviously a model or something similar.

Feeling quite out of my depth and in alien territory, I had this confirmed to me by the aforementioned singing star, who closed the door in my face accompanied by the words, 'No. You're not,' when I enquired whether I was supposed to share the dressing-room he had just entered.

'Not to worry,' I thought, meandering down the corridor, hoping that someone would come and tell me what I was supposed to be doing. A few moments later I was rescued, given a cup of tea and introduced to Damien, the producer, who was very welcoming and went over the ground that we had covered on the phone. He then took me to meet the horses and their owners, which was where the fun began.

There were two families who had brought three horses between them. I don't know where Damien had found them but one party had left home at 4.30 in order to arrive in London at 6 in the morning. Their horse was immaculately groomed and I fell for him straightaway. To me he shone out as a racehorse, but right now he had 'show horse' written all over him. His owners were clearly sceptical of my abilities and, although polite, were very uncertain. It eluded me as to why or, moreover, how they had been enticed to come. Perhaps it was the lure of television. But their horse was beautiful.

The second trailer had two occupants, both belonging to children. I was a little concerned by this as I duly recognised the underlying poor health of the Shetland belonging to the young son. I have a continual internal crisis about children's ponies because I shall never forget the adoration I had for mine. Had someone told me then that something was amiss with one of my ponies, and that it was potentially serious, I would have been devastated. This constantly plays on my mind whenever I am asked to look at a child's pony, and here I was now with two of them. I said a silent prayer in hope that the parents were already aware of the Shetland's state of health.

By now the dawn was beginning to break and, although cold, it looked as if a glorious bright sky would see us through the programme. I was delighted, but some of the professionals were not. It seemed that some equipment for one of the games to be played in the garden was under threat of explosion, or worse, if the sun shone on it. This brought people flooding from the house, trailing wires, clutching clipboards, shrieking into microphones and bellowing orders. With the exception of one or two, they all had cigarettes dangling from their mouths.

I paused long enough to take in this sight which was well worthwhile since it brought everything into perspective for me. It was clear that, without doubt, the horses and I were the only sane parties here. From what I was witnessing, the others were so manic that I wasn't out of my depth at all. I had expected serene, professional competence. I'm not sure why. To my relief the reality was very different: a huge, tall man, heavily made up to look like a woman; a

TV 'celeb' looking as if his world had just fallen apart because his game might be scrapped; assorted budding dancers standing shivering, barefoot on the cold wet grass, the males clad in shorts, the girls in skimpy bikinis – surrounded by people in sheepskin coats, hats, scarfs and gloves. I felt decidedly normal. All my worries about being thought of as strange, melted away. The only thing I had to contend with now were the horses' owners.

There was one small hitch which, it appeared, had gone unnoticed. The horses were required to be in the garden. The only way into the garden was across the canal via a narrow concrete bridge with two metal handrails on either side, supported by steel runners through the concrete.

It posed no problem for the Shetland who would have happily trundled back and forwards all day. He was enjoying his day out. His stablemate, a larger pony mare was uncertain but her young owner was determined that she should cross. She backed off, urged forwards by the little girl. Watching, I experienced another dilemma. On one hand I fully understood the excitement of the children. It was a thrill for them to be on the show, would probably become a cherished memory and would certainly bring them great 'street-cred' among their friends. But my real understanding went out to the horses.

The Shetland found it easy to cross. Yes, because of his size, but also because of his inborn ability to lower his eyeline. By dropping his line of vision below his great bushy forelock he could cast a shadow that made it easy for him to see where he was going. His slightly high, flicky knee action meant that his own footfalls did not interfere with his line of vision, which is why Shetlands take short, choppy steps and go around with their heads down. They are very natural creatures, with a sound understanding of vibration and great sensitivity to their environment; they turn their bottoms to bad weather and face into good. The sun, now rising ahead of him, did not conflict with his natural instincts – animals in the wild migrate towards the sun for food and warmth. The particular resonance of the concrete bridge vibrating through his unshod feet, told him that the bridge was strong enough for him to cross.

The mare, being about 14hh, was not so well off. Encouraged again by the young girl she walked very happily onto the bridge, and very quickly stopped, about to go into reverse but prevented from doing so by the parents.

She looked straight at me. I knew that look but I could offer no advice because I understood how the bridge felt to her. Because she had had an accident at some stage and damaged her back, the sensation in her hind limbs was diminished, so now she relied heavily upon the sensation in her forelimbs. As she had walked onto the bridge the resonance of her metal shoes had sent a strong vibration along the bridge which would have suggested it to be solid enough. Unfortunately, with the metal handrails either side and the connecting metal runners attached to the underside, the whole ensemble acted like a massive tuning fork.

As she tested the safety of the bridge with her forefeet, the resonance came back through the handrails and went through her. The effect for her was the same as that which we experience from mild static electricity, only in her case it was hitting her sensitive muzzle. As soon as she felt this, she responded appropriately by backing off, the message being: 'There is no way through. Your way is barred.' She gamefully tried again, but it happened yet again.

I fully understood her plight but did not feel that now was the appropriate time to get into a debate and try to explain what was happening to the owners. All that they had deduced was that she was excited, and that the bridge was a little narrow, but that with a bit of firmness she would go over. They brought back the Shetland to give her a lead.

I stood by and watched, silent and not doing a great deal in the way of whispering. To the respective owners it must have seemed that I was pretty hopeless with the practicalities of dealing with horses. Hopefully I would be better at talking to them or the whole scenario would turn out to be a disaster. Had I been one of them, I probably would have agreed with their opinions. But I wasn't, and now I stood in awe watching the two ponies help each other.

The larger pony moved close behind her stable mate, the Shetland, and pressed her nose into the top of his tail. This muffled the vibration coming from the metal handrail for her and he was only too happy to allow her to do this. In order to accommodate her need to take large, solid steps with her forelimbs, he proceeded at a very quick jog, unfortunately squashing the mare's owner who had tried to make room for herself where there wasn't any. Pulling the mare back from the Shetland, the little girl made herself the substitute without realising it. The pony buried her nose in the child's back and ushered her across the bridge. Sadly, her common sense earned her one or two reprimands rather than praise, but so be it. She had done it, with the help of her Shetland friend – and not an auditory sound or visible sign passed between them. There was no way that I could compete with the wisdom and help imparted to the little mare by the Shetland. 'He's the one they should interview,' I thought, 'not me.'

Two across, one to go. Alf, the big horse, was brought to the bridge but was having none of it. He wouldn't go within seven yards of the bridge, planting his feet and raising his head in a determined 'NO'. You didn't need any whispering skills to interpret that one.

Mr Alf, in no way perturbed by his horse's defiant stance, joined in the game by adopting a counter-posture, squaring up to Alf with his chest out, elbows and knees bent and his chin tucked into his neck, looking him straight in the eye. Unfortunately, he then made a huge tactical error. Napoleon Bonaparte would have been horrified. His stance was perfect, his aura solid, portraying nothing but conviction, but he walked away! He walked in the opposite direction! From Alf's perspective it must have been like climbing into the ring with Chris Eubank and having him strut his stuff right past you and out of the fire exit. Unbelievable!

But wait, Mr Alf was advancing again, now armed with various bits of tackle. He had been to the trailer for reinforcements. Things were looking up. Unfortunately, from the horse's point of view, Mr and Mrs Alf, in their enthusiasm, hadn't quite managed to grasp the rules of the game and were making them up as they went along. The horse looked round to see what the next move would be. Mrs Alf's immediate response was to begin a war dance on the end of the reins, tugging on the bit and trying to keep his head straight in an attempt to distract him from his opponent. Not fair play.

Mr Alf, at this point, marched purposefully along the right flank of the enemy, employing goading tactics, obviously assuming that his opponent required stronger encouragement. Squaring his shoulders even more, arms full of tackle, elbows perpendicular to his sides, one eye closed, he turned the full glare of the still open eye, his left, directly at the back of Alf's right ear.

Holding this priceless pose for a moment or two, he then surprised everyone by swiftly pivoting on one foot, dropping his torso to ground level and raising his buttocks in a very determined manner towards Alf. With one deft movement, he whipped out a rope from the tangle of paraphernalia and secured it firmly to the base of the bridge.

At this point, I offered my services. Mrs Alf ceased her applaudable war dance and became the pillar of social propriety. 'Yes, of course,' she said with a smile, handing me the reins.

Mr Alf looked briefly crestfallen and thwarted. He stood, battle stance at the ready, somewhat precariously positioned on the right flank. He had his strategy and that was that.

I tried to restore some semblance of fair play. I felt the horse to be outnumbered. With the reins held loosely in my right hand, standing on his left side, I dropped my right shoulder down and back, moved my left shoulder forward, stretching my left arm slightly away from my body and the battle scene. Now I had adopted the same posture as Alf, indicating that I was on his side, and that I understood what he was doing.

I glanced briefly at Alf, at his eye, then at his nose. It's so much more polite to talk to the nostril. 'Do you trust me?' I asked.

Instantly he lowered his head, pricked his ears and turned in my direction. Yes, he did.

Courteously, I turned away. Standing like this, with the back of my head towards him, my thoughts were so much more readily received. He duly responded by turning his head away from me. Bliss! Like this we could eat together, protect each other, and converse in an uninterrupted way.

I was in love. The bridge didn't matter, the programme didn't matter, nothing mattered except the emotional feelings of this horse. They were all consuming and enveloping; like a hot shower, a delicious liqueur, and toasting one's feet in front of a roaring fire, all rolled into one. I was in heaven. I'd known I would fall for this horse the moment I'd seen him. Now I knew why. He was Horse, pure Horse, and nothing but Horse. In spite of the 17 or so years of schooling, re-education, training and competing – all to serve *our* needs – he had never lost himself. He was all heart.

Mr Alf poured icy water on my dream. 'We've tried it your way, now let's try the conventional method, shall we?'

A battle cry of 'Charge!' if ever I'd heard one. Suddenly I felt very sad. Not in a visible external way but with an inner sorrow.

I glanced at Alf, catching his eye and his thought, 'They do it all the time.' No malice, no judgement, no bitterness, just sadness – as one might be terribly philosophical about a primitive species. Sad, but accepting: *it's just their way.*

Mrs Alf, who must have felt very sorry for me at this stage, my moment of glory having just gone up in smoke, very kindly said, 'Don't worry about it, dear. He does this all the time. It's the same every time we travel him.' So entrenched were they in their war games, each with a different set of rules, that they couldn't see the wood for the trees.

I left them at this point, beckoned by Damien. Time was getting on; it was 7.10. Oh, hell. What was I going to do with this lot in front of a live audience in a chaotic studio?

I needn't have worried. The demo went down a treat. I whizzed my way through the three horses with as much gusto as I could muster, dishing out bits of information that the respective owners would recognise as having come from their horses, accompanied by Mark Little – whom I could only see as Joe Mangel, having been a *Neighbours* fan.

I had been concerned that I would fall into a melting heap when standing next to a TV celebrity who I had watched avidly for some years, but my love for Alf won the day. There was no contest. As I stood beside Alf, his nose in my hand, his elegant head pressed against me, Mark Little was the runner-up all the way.

All that worry 24 hours earlier seemed like a dream now. The owners were friendly as we chatted over breakfast, courtesy of the programme; the children hungry and thrilled with everything, including their ponies. It was all over. 'Or is it?' I wondered. 'How much influence does television carry?'

I was about to find out.

6

Aristotle

The live screening of *The Big Breakfast* coincided with the report of a blind trial of my abilities published in *Your Horse* magazine. Their write-up was extremely favourable, and now the calls came flooding in. We were absolutely inundated with pleas for help and requests for visits from needy owners and their horses. Letters also arrived, from as far afield as South Africa, Australia, America and Cyprus, accompanying the hundreds of enquiries made by people in this country.

Robert and I were amazed by the response, and totally unprepared for the onslaught. We did our very best to accommodate everyone who called. Sitting in the end bedroom of the caravan, among the ever-filling pots and pans of rainwater, we answered the constantly ringing phone, sent faxes, set up files, organised visits, plotted routes, and hastily ran to and from the yard to see to our own horses.

Suddenly finding myself so sought-after was quite a shock to my system and brought with it a new direction. A change in my focus had to coincide accordingly. To date, my communication with horses had always been for them; what they needed or wanted. Now, it had to be much more for the people; their needs and their wants from their animals.

I felt from the word go that this might prove a mite difficult for me as, historically, I had always put the needs of animals above those of humans. I had recently stipulated this, in no uncertain terms, to a lady reporter from a national newspaper who had sought me out for an interview on behalf of her editor.

The said reporter was keen on a story but had an ulterior motive, namely that she was desperately seeking someone who could tell her daughter's up-and-coming eventer to 'jolly well pull itself together and make sure it gets daughter to the regional finals'. This type of thing I do not do. Nor is it in any sense appropriate behaviour for me. As a consequence I did not get my interview published; it lies to this day in a dark drawer somewhere, gathering dust and cobwebs.

Nevertheless, the whole publicity surge gave me a much greater insight into other people's relationships with their horses than I could ever have experienced without it.

One of my very first visits was to a very nice lady with a horse who had shared her life for some 18 years. They had obviously been through nearly everything together and knew each other extremely well. As June relayed their history over the phone, it was not immediately apparent to me how I could help. Then she came to the crux. It was the biting, you see. He had always been a bit of a rogue, and quite difficult with a mind of his own, but somehow they had always managed to muddle through. She had always believed that the biting would improve with age, but on reflection, after all these years, he seemed not to have improved at all; if anything, he had got worse. Would I come and see him?

'Er, yes. Of course,' was my reply, wondering how on earth I was going to break the habit of an entire lifetime during a one-hour visit. A few choice words perhaps: 'Stop it, and stop it now!' or 'Please don't bite any more. Thank you.' Maybe something to the effect of, 'Biting is unacceptable at your age. Grow up.'

I duly arrived to meet a very excited June, a little after the appointed time. (Most of my clients would probably agree that my lateness is more of a trademark of mine than anything else.)

'Oh, it's just so wonderful to meet you. I can't believe that you've come. I'm so excited!' trilled June, hurrying along the drive to meet me.

Greetings such as this always leave me stuck for words, never quite sure how to live up to the expectations of the greeter. To me, it's the horses that are amazing, not me, but people don't always want to know this.

Anyway, here I was, my arrival heralded as though that of a great stateswoman, being ceremoniously ushered in the direction of the stables, situated just left of June's bungalow. Walking up the steep driveway from the lower courtyard, I noticed how the buildings melted beautifully into the side of the cliff-like hill, and tried to concentrate on listening to June.

She was in full flow, telling me of an incident which had occurred when her horse was five and he'd smashed the stable door to pieces; of another when he was seven and had taken off with her in the woods, flinging her into a group of holly bushes – deliberately, of that there was no doubt in her mind. Another time she had taken him on holiday with her and he had been impeccably behaved, right up to the moment when he'd blotted his copybook completely by taking a great chunk out of a passing tourist.

While these helpful insights were being relayed to me, my eyes were taking in the makeshift fencing which lined the drive all the way to the yard – rows of thin metal sheep-fencing stakes, held upright by neat strands of baler twine carefully knotted together. The same type of barrier surrounded an oval lawn and flower-bed which served as a turning circle at the end of the gravelled drive. The once beautifully manicured lawn now sported great gouged-out hoofprints. At first glance I was unsure just how big this dangerous, demented creature would turn out to be since the enormous hoofmarks indicated something akin to a Clydesdale. Aristotle was, however, one of the finer breeds – dare I say it, a thoroughbred.

Passing his turn-out paddock, I marvelled again at the fencing; a little sturdier here but consisting of an assortment of timber in varying sizes, textures and colours. What alarmed me, however, were the interspersed lengths of plastic water piping tied on with the inevitable baler twine.

Noting my surprise at these, June quickly explained. 'Well, it's the biting, you see. I have to use indestructable materials or things that can be replaced quickly and easily – cheaply too, you know. Baler twine is marvellous. I use quite a lot of it, you know. Now, come and meet Aristotle. He'll be delighted to see you, I'm sure.'

Her steps hastened as we approached the darkened interior of a stable door. No ordinary door this. It was heavily reinforced with what could only be described as army surplus armour-plating; a metal buttress, hugely dented, riveted to the top of it.

'I'm sure he'll be delighted to see me too,' I replied, wondering whether I came under the category of indestructible or replaceable.

Suddenly, there he was, all 17.2hh of him, appearing as if by magic, framed in the doorway. Jet black himself, he was barely visible against the dark interior of the stable except for a huge pair of snapping yellow teeth and the whites of his rolling eyes, also with a distinctly yellow tinge to them.

June was ready, though, and sprang into action. Laying a hand with one swift, deft movement to a strategically placed rod of Alcathene piping, she quickly brought calm to what, she clearly believed, could have been a very nasty incident.

'Get back, you brute!' she bellowed, timing her command

beautifully to coincide with a series of swinging blows to the jaws of this crazed creature. 'Get back!' *Whack! Whack! Whack!*

Alcathene piping makes a strange 'zinging' sound when swung through the air at great speed. Very useful stuff – seemingly indestructible, yet light to wield. I could envisage June demonstrating the uses of this wonderful material to a large audience of prospective buyers, if ever the need arose. She clearly prided herself on her resourcefulness and had stumbled upon this innovative equine tool quite by chance.

Zing, whack! Zing-zing, whack! 'I show him no fear, you see!' topped with one final 'zing, whack', just for good measure.

'That's better,' she said in a satisfied tone. 'Shall I put his headcollar on now?'

'Umm, er, yes – if you like.' I was a little dumbfounded. Perhaps she had been given the wrong phone number and thought that I was Mary Chipperfield.

Armed with her plastic life-saving sword, June advanced with a heavy-duty leather headcollar. Although the door was now open, there was still not sufficient light for me to catch more than a glimpse of the occupant. I could just make out that he was tall and was seemingly growing taller as June loomed at him with the headcollar.

'Now stop that!' she yelled. There followed another bout of 'zing-zing, whack!'

I waited patiently outside the door, catching fleeting glimpses of rug buckles, the odd flash of a shod hoof, and the yellowed white of an eye. The tussle continued, sounds of 'zing, whack! zing, whack!' filling the air.

Suddenly, all went quiet. June emerged triumphant, albeit a little rosy-cheeked and looking somewhat dishevelled.

'I show him no fear, you know. I'm sure that's best. Do go in. I'm dying to know what you're going to say.'

'So am I,' I thought, entering the lion's den. It was so dark that I couldn't see him at first, but as my eyes became accustomed to the darkness, I found him – secured very firmly by a thick chain, double-looped through his headcollar and back to a ring in the wall.

He was big, but size is not something which worries me so I moved closer, still peering through the gloom. Normally I stand quietly, still myself, and wait for the horse to offer some form of communication first. In light of what I had just witnessed, I felt that this would definitely be the best approach for Aristotle. A little space and calmness would be good for him.

Unfortunately, June had other ideas. In her excitement, she could wait no longer than 30 seconds. 'Look! I'll show you what he does,' she said marching round to his front end. Turning her back to his jaws, she attempted to unfasten the rug buckles at his chest. He took a swipe.

'Arrgh! You see? He got me!' she exclaimed with genuine surprise.

I was surprised; surprised that June should be so surprised. She looked at me expectantly, clearly waiting for some pearl of horse whispering wisdom to issue forth from my lips to change her life and clamp these clashing jaws shut forever more.

Sadly, I had to disappoint her. Nothing immediately sprang to mind.

'Could I have a moment or two alone with him, please?' I asked. After a brief pause she agreed, retreating to attend to the important task of replacing worn baler twine with new.

As I stood there alone with Aristotle, I was struck by a profound sense of anguish, enormous anguish. One minute, I had been perfectly happy; the next, this anguish had descended like a great wave of filthy water laden with oil, litter and old cigarette butts, sent up by a double-decker bus as it splashed through a puddle. I was swamped. I felt as though I'd been grabbed by the throat and tied at the knees by this anguish. Anguish is the only word I can use since it encompasses a whole range of emotions: anger, fear, frustration, despair – all jumbled up and rolled into one. At that moment, I felt as if my mind had been through a fast wash cycle – a mental roller-coaster.

'Okay,' I spoke without words, 'I understand. Slow down and explain.'

Aristotle looked round. His eyes were pleading; begging and pleading. 'Stop it! Stop it! Stop it!' Far from the soft responses I normally get from horses, this chap was like a sledgehammer. The force of his message was like having cymbals crashing beside my ears, much more akin to the time when Arnie blasted me with his toothache.

I was taken aback. Firstly I had been subjected to June and now to her horse. It was proving to be a draining experience and I had barely begun. Aside from this, I have never been able to prevent myself from becoming completely involved with anyone or anything in distress, be it person, horse, dog or even an upturned beetle. Attempting to gather myself together as best I could, I took a deep breath.

'Show me. Show me what's the matter,' I said. His response was dramatic, powerful, and very explicit. He swung his head down, gnashing at his chest. Then lifting and snaking his neck out, massive

68

jaws wide open, he clamped his teeth around the metal ring in the wall, locking his jaws like a pit bull terrier and swivelling his eyes to look straight at me. Suddenly I heard June returning. So, too, did Aristotle.

'How are you two getting along?' she sang as she approached the stable.

Without loosing his grip on the metal ring, Aristotle took matters into his own hands, figuratively speaking, of course. He swung his great hulking quarters at me, shoving me in no uncertain terms across the stable. Surprised, left floundering and out of balance, I received another shove. Now I was up against the wall, squashed by his bulk, my face buried in his left flank. I managed to unmuffle my face and turn my head, just in time to see June parade in.

'Oh, my goodness! You naughty boy!' came her horrified reproach. 'Just you get off her right now!'

Simultaneously I received another sledgehammer blow of Aristotle's anguish: 'Don't go! Stay!'

'Really, June, it's all right,' I stuttered, from my cramped position between Aristotle's rear-end and the wall. Desperately rifling through my mind for the words to explain, I was not given the opportunity.

June was not listening. Seizing his tail she gave it a hefty tug and yanked him off me. 'There. Do you see what he's like? He's so terribly naughty.'

I interjected, 'Well, no, June. He's not naughty at all actually. He's much more desperate than that.'

June was still not listening and continued to express her dismay to Aristotle about his behaviour – and in no uncertain terms. 'You are a brute – such a brute! I told you not to behave like this yet you keep doing it time and time again. I'm really at my wits' end with you. Why can't you behave yourself just for once?'

June was beside herself. I thought for a moment that she was going to burst into floods of frustrated tears and I couldn't help but feel sorry for her.

She continued. 'This nice young lady has come to help you and all you can do is squash her.'

Aristotle, still retaining his terrier-like grip on the metal ring, gave her a facial snarl. Watching the pair of them was like witnessing an antagonistic married couple all but throwing tins at each other in a supermarket.

I tried again. 'Now June. You must understand . . .'

I was cut short. Aristotle, relinquishing his grip on the ring, swung his head round at great speed, and with his great jaws gaping wide open, snaked cobra-like at June. Still tied by the chain, short but very strong, he was denied his taste of flesh. Not to be outdone, he raised one huge forelimb and brought it smashing to the ground with a mighty thud. Still not content, he followed up with a scything lash of his thick tail, catching our June a hefty blow around the midriff. Fortunately she was wearing something thick enough to afford a buffer. Any of you who have been swiped with a tail on bare flesh will know exactly what I mean.

June was momentarily silent, her own jaws agape. Aristotle, however, had not finished. With one deft sideways movement, he caught June with his quarters, sending her flying against the wall where I was still standing. Another great shove from his bottom, and I found myself pressed firmly back against the wall embracing June in a most intimate manner! I, being a good deal shorter than she, now had my face buried deep in her bosom, while June's jaw rested very snugly on the top of my head, both of us held firmly in place by Aristotle's great hindquarters.

Finally June spoke. 'I think it's best I turn him out now.' I knew exactly what she meant; to suggest that it was becoming a little cramped in the stable would have undoubtedly been an understatement.

With a great deal of wriggling, uttering polite apologies to one another, we managed to disentangle ourselves – although, I have to say, only by the grace of Aristotle who could have held us there indefinitely had he so wished.

'I'll just go and get his New Zealand rug,' said June, making a swift exit. She returned promptly, rug over one arm and Alcathene pipe in the opposite hand. 'Now we'll have *no* more of your nonsense!' She spoke with renewed authority. Brandishing her plastic pipe aloft as though a sword, she advanced on Aristotle. At this point he was looking a little more relaxed, merely scraping his teeth across his wrought-iron manger, but the advance of June brought a resurgence of his earlier fraught behaviour.

Zing, whack! Zing, whack! 'Gertcha!' growled June. Much stomping, flailing and gnashing ensued. Amid this, June succeeded in swapping Aristotle's day rug for his turn-out rug. She also succeeded in unchaining him and attaching a lead rope to his headcollar. Now he had June's right arm in his sights as a substitute for the metal wall ring. Moving her arm swiftly, she managed to keep it – and I mean literally keep it. Aristotle, meanwhile, was dissuaded from further attack in the short term by the threatening gestures made by the plastic pipe held in June's left hand.

Suddenly June's attention was diverted. 'Oh my goodness! I've forgotten to fence off the drive. Here. Would you mind holding him for a minute?' She handed the end of the lead rope to me and made for the door.

Aristotle, desperate now for freedom and fresh air, followed in hot pursuit. June beat him to it and swung the stable door shut with a hefty bang, dealing him another blow on the neck with her pipe at the same time. 'Get back, you bugger!'

'Won't be a moment,' she called to me over her shoulder as she set off down the drive – leaving me alone in the stable, on the inside of the heavily reinforced extra high door – with Aristotle!

I had hold of his lead rope but it was completely ineffectual. Aristotle went into a fury; screaming and roaring, ramming his chest against the door, stamping his front legs up and down, and cracking his knees against the door frame, while I stood beside him watching his great 17.2hh bulk wind up like a powder keg about to blow. The door creaked and groaned, bulged and strained under the force of Aristotle's weight as he flung himself against it. He paused briefly from his throaty cries only to sink his great yellow teeth into the metal plate riveted to the top of the door.

All I could think at the time was, 'I've left my car in the drive – surely she doesn't mean to fence it off with baler twine!' Meanwhile, Aristotle continued his loud tirade.

June returned. 'Now just you watch this!' she exclaimed, heaving him back from the door. 'This is when he gets really dangerous!'

As she unbolted the door, it flew back crashing against the wall – and out he came, scattering his legs in all directions and gouging even deeper holes in the gravel. Taking great open-jawed swipes at the plastic pipe held in June's hand, he made a well-timed grab and got it. Said pipe locked firmly in his teeth, he reared, standing up on his hind legs, nearly wrenching June's arm from its socket. Neither lost their grip; his vice-like, hers more or less equal to his. He returned to earth, crashing his great hooves into the drive, then, again, he went up, retaining his lockjaw hold on the piping which, seemingly, had lost all its power of control since leaving the stable.

This was how Aristotle progressed his way to the field; surprisingly respectful of the single strand of baler twine marking the route, he hauled and jiggled June up and down by her left arm, occasionally shaking his head on the upward thrust of a rear for good measure.

On reaching the field entrance, a final tussle ensued for ownership of the pipe. It turned out to be a dead-heat – both of them let go at the same time and Aristotle set off at a thunderous pace to the bottom of the paddock. June retrieved her trusty, but now muddied, plastic sword – which, it must be said, had ably demonstrated the near-indestructible qualities of Alcathene – and began to put the sliprails up across the gap.

And just in the nick of time too, for Aristotle, having reached the bottom of the paddock very swiftly indeed, had spun round and was now setting an impressive pace back up. On the approach, his ears pricked giving his face a reasonably pleasant expression. Then five yards out they flattened alarmingly and his enormous jaws gaped wide yet again. Once again, he managed to get a lock on his target – this time, fortunately, the wooden rail that June had just seconds before slid into its keeper. Three hefty great bites were taken in quick succession while the sound of splintering wood reverberated around us.

I seized the opportunity – June was at this point quiet. 'Now then June, you must understand that he does actually have some physical problems, and quite severe ones too. They are not going to be that easy to help but I feel I must explain to you how he is feeling, preferably before one of you gets killed.' I chose my words deliberately; sometimes saying something attention-grabbing does the trick and gets the point across – but not in the case of June.

'Oh yes, that would be lovely,' she cooed. 'I can't tell you how lovely it is to have you here – so wonderful of you to come. And you get on *so* well with him. Now let's go and have a nice cup of tea and some cake.'

I turned to look at Aristotle who had paused from his frantic wood devouring and who now stood quietly with ears pricked, looking at me. I shrugged my shoulders at him. 'I'll give it my best shot,' I told him under my breath.

And so I described to June his multiple physical ailments – pains and aches in his back, his neck, his legs, his feet, and strains and stresses in his muscles. As I talked, she marvelled: 'Oh my goodness, yes. Now I remember – he would have done that when I had a crash and overturned his trailer'; 'Of course, now that you mention it he did go funny on that leg after we fell in a ditch'; 'Aha – yes, that would make sense. His neck has never been right since he took a tumble with me on the road.'

And so the list went on. Aristotle was a walking battlefield. Frankly,

I was amazed that he still resembled a horse. By now I had June's full attention and so I gave her the details of an excellent homoeopathic vet in her area with whom I had worked on many occasions. He would definitely be able to help with some of the problems.

I went on further to explain to June the reasons behind Aristotle's biting. At some point in his early life, prior to meeting June, Aristotle had done himself a serious mischief. As a result, his senses had gone haywire, although he had probably always been a sensitive horse – sensitive to all external impressions; sight, sound, taste, touch and vibration.

This hypersensitivity was the cause of his whole series of accidents. The acuteness of his senses was intolerable; sounds were too loud and distorted; his sensitivity to touch was so pronounced that it was painful – he had an awareness of practically every nerve in his whole body, resulting in him feeling as if he were being pricked by a million pins; his vision was so distorted that he could not focus properly; and finally all the nerves in his upper and lower jaws felt as though they were on fire.

The only way he felt able to alleviate the pains was to hit them really hard or to apply great pressure to afford himself some form of relief. This was why he clamped his teeth, vice-like, around everything imaginable; this was why he slammed his feet into the ground; this was why he bashed his hindquarters against the walls – he was literally being driven mad by his own body. Every sound coursed through his senses like someone scraping their fingernails down a blackboard, every touch grated through his bones, every step he took shot electric-type spasms up his limbs. This had been Aristotle's life for 20-odd years!

June, bless her heart, had persevered. Down through the years she had picked herself up off the tarmac on more than one occasion, bathed her various cuts and bruises, and soothed the endless bite marks. She had fed him, cherished him, and loved him throughout 18 years of strife. In spite of everything, he was still her 'best friend in all the world', as she put it.

For 18 years she had cried, wailed and sobbed tears of grief and frustration; she had flown into rages of anger and confusion; she had survived being flung into trees, bushes and ditches. In return she had let him graze on her precious lawn, taken him on holiday with her, and ridden him bareback to the beach.

She loved him. She would never give up loving him. And Aristotle loved her – who else would have tolerated his extremes of behaviour?

His greatest fear was that one day June would leave; that one day he would go too far. He couldn't help what he did. His body punished him mercilessly every moment of every day. June had on more than one occasion threatened him with being sold – or worse. Yet she had never meant it, had never loved him any less throughout all the mutual bashings and bruisings and beatings.

Aristotle didn't need me – or Mary Chipperfield. Aristotle needed June.

7

Hector's Voice

I pulled into the long driveway, amazingly enough on time for my next appointment, my fourth so far that day. This was no mean feat since the drive entrance had been well and truly hidden between two brick walls, and heavily disguised by a large willow tree and a telephone box. These landmarks had been very clearly mentioned to me when I had been given the directions but I had not expected them to be situated all together, hiding the entrance.

Directions are very strange things. During the many thousands of miles that I was to drive on my visits, I managed, on the whole, to find the majority of locations, although some did elude me altogether. Many of the directions given to me were peculiar. Driving along strange roads looking for landmarks causes problems within problems.

Sometimes great swathes of countryside were missed out of directions altogether; entire villages did not exist, junctions and crossroads were not mentioned, yet tree stumps and phone boxes featured in abundance, as did painted stones and panelled fences.

On one particular occasion, on a very wet and stormy autumnal afternoon, after having driven round endlessly in circles looking for a spectacularly elusive lane somewhere on my left, I had to pull over and call from my mobile phone. Relieved to hear the voice of my client on the other end of the line, I explained to her carefully, and in great detail, that I was parked by a small conglomeration of shops: newsagent, off-licence, grocer, and launderette, by which there was a set of pedestrian lights. I described, also, the village green and public house situated on the other side of the road.

'Oh,' she had replied, 'I think I know where you are, but I'm hopeless with directions. I'll just go and get my husband.'

I then relayed the information to her husband, again in the same detail, to which had come the resounding reply, 'Oh great! You're not far away at all. Just keep going straight on for about a quarter of a mile and you can't miss us. We're just on the left by the puddle. See you in a minute. We'll be looking out for you.' And with that, he'd rung off!

'By the puddle!' I'd repeated to myself, phone in hand, peering out of the car window at the streaming, lashing rain, pouring out of the sky and forming numerous great pools of water on the tarmac. 'Turn left by the puddle,' I'd mused, scratching my head in disbelief . . .

Getting out of the car now at Melissa's yard, memories came flooding back to me. It was a little makeshift yard behind a row of houses. An arena lay on the left, running alongside the drive and surfaced in wood shavings, which were currently only visible as tufts sticking up out of the frost-packed ground. Ahead of me were gates leading to five acres of grazing, split into three paddocks. Barbed-wire fencing, glazed with frost, twinkled in the bright winter sunshine. The stables were three in number, purpose built with a walkway separating them from the arena. At the far end of these, a lean-to garage had been divided by partitions to create two further stables; sliprails served as doors, and great piles of clean, golden straw spilled out over the walkway which was beginning to defrost in patches.

Melissa rented the yard and made her living from teaching people to ride, improving horses for people, buying youngsters and selling them on, and finding horses on behalf of clients. She worked on her own, and just by looking at the little yard, it was obvious that she threw her heart and soul into it. I remembered, only too well, my own experiences in this area: the endless hours of hard work, the juggling of expenses and running costs to make ends meet – never losing my adoration for the horses and wanting nothing but the very best for them.

This, too, was Melissa. She chose her clients carefully; sympathetic and genuine people who cared about the horses as well as wishing to learn to ride them. She found horses which were waifs and strays, surplus to the requirements of others, and provided them with everything that she possibly could. She spent every waking moment looking after them and tending to them, whilst still looking for ways to expand the business and make it pay; yet all the time never over-using her horses in lessons, and perhaps, in part, not wishing them to be used at all.

Melissa was lovely – very honest, very genuine, and very friendly. She survived, much as I do, on an endless succession of cups of tea and cigarettes. Her main concern was Hector. When she spoke about him, her face lit up and displayed her passion for him. She explained to me how beautifully he worked in the arena, how amazing he was with novice riders, how forgiving he was, and how generous. In short, he was her best horse, her pride and joy.

As we chatted over a cup of tea, she told me gently that she had no problems with him being as grumpy as he was in the stable, providing that she knew he was happy. He had bitten her quite hard at times, not often, but often enough. As far as his work was concerned, he was an absolute gem, but when it came to being friends in the stable, something was very amiss; he would make faces, and even chase her out from time to time. Melissa reiterated that if that was just his way, then so be it – she loved him just the same – but if he had a problem, or needed help, then whatever he wanted, he could have.

'Okay,' I said. 'I'll go and ask him.' It was so refreshing to meet someone who was so open to what I could do, so completely clear of scepticism, or a need to challenge or trap me. I really appreciated it.

I invited myself into Hector's stable. He stared straight at me – big handsome face, large ears, slightly Roman nose. He held this gaze for a split second then ran to the corner of his stable, hiding his head in it. I stood very still and quiet, immediately feeling very sorry for him. 'What's up, Hector?' I asked gently and out loud. A mere flick of an ear – an almost imperceptible twitch, but nothing else. He stayed firmly planted in the corner, head in the shadows. He was giving nothing away so I assumed that maybe he was shy or something.

I turned slightly away from him, facing in the opposite direction, and explained simply who I was, and why I was there. I told him everything that Melissa had said about him, how much of a star he was for her, and how she wasn't angry with him, just very concerned and upset to see him like this. I explained that she wanted to help him in any way that she could, and all he needed to do was say what he wanted.

I spoke softly, aloud, and in detail. Then, I waited. And waited. And waited. Nothing. Hector just stood very still in his corner. So I waited some more. Still nothing. I felt terrible and desperately sorry for him. He was so stiff and tense, and so completely immobile. He made me feel as if I were the worst kind of headmistress.

I reached out my hand and stroked him very gently on the neck. He jumped, tense and shaky. This was awful. I could understand exactly how Melissa felt. It is perhaps the worst feeling in the world to have a horse, or anyone for that matter, cowering away from you in a corner. I felt close to tears, but thought that it would hardly be of benefit to Hector to have me blubbering away in his stable.

So I tried, yet again. 'Hector, whatever it is, you can be honest. It will be okay. It's soul destroying seeing you like this. Is there nothing that we can do to help?'

He glanced at me briefly, moving his head but a fraction of an inch in my direction, then back to the corner again; troubled, and tense, and rock-still, standing to attention. I felt that the best thing that I could do was go back to Melissa and explain, extend her the same honesty that she had me. If I couldn't help, then so be it. I was sad though – I can't bear to see anything like that. I explained to Hector that this was what I was going to do, more as a last-ditch attempt to get him to reply. But he didn't.

I left the stable quietly, and turned around to bolt the door. At that point, I got the shock of my life. Hector flew with lightning speed from his traumatised position in the corner, shot his head over the stable door, and latched himself onto my throat! Both my hands were still attached to the door bolt, but my eyes were locked with his, his teeth still firmly harnessed to my throat. Luckily, due to the cold weather, I had a thick scarf on and my winter jacket buttoned right up to the top of my neck. His eyes were what concerned me the most. They contained rage – absolute, blind, furious rage – the like of which one rarely sees. I could only assume that this was what it would be like to be a burglar confronted by a Rottweiler. The rage was meant: so venomous, so pure, and so very real. It is widely stated that the eyes are the windows to the soul. If so, then Hector's soul was in serious trouble!

He let go as quickly as he had grabbed me, and flew back to the far corner of the stable again. I stood very still; I had not taken my hands off the bolt. On reflection, this was quite surprising. I would have expected my hands to have defended me in some way but they had not. In that moment of stillness, clarity spread over me like the sunbeams reaching across the frost.

Hector had been the victim of ignorant abuse at some stage – by whom, or in what manner, I was not aware. But it had left him with a deep, deep personal sense of anger, resentment, and mortification; an all-consuming fire burning in his soul. Disbelief, shock, and wounded hurt, fed and nurtured there – moment by moment, hour by hour, day by day, month by month, year by year – until the feeling became a smouldering furnace, stoked and calmed, stoked and calmed, until it could be contained no longer. Then it broke free and roared, like a grumbling volcano suddenly bursting through the earth's crust and showering a searing, molten fury way up into the atmosphere, spewing and belching a great mass of fire.

He needed to do this; he couldn't help it. This burning, seething, deep-seated poison would kill him if he didn't let it go. But how could he fully let it go? He adored Melissa, knew that everything she did was for him. Her life revolved around him, and the other horses, of course, but he was her particular favourite. He understood only too well her adoration for him; he felt the warmth and glow from her whenever she watched him work; he felt the love with which she mixed his feeds, mucked out his stable, groomed him, and tucked him into his rugs. He loved her with just as much passion in return. Yet he held inside him this rage, this historic fury, belonging to another time, another place, and other people – not Melissa.

What could he do? How could he free himself without alarming, frightening, or hurting her? He couldn't. And so he swallowed it, pushing it deep within, way, way back into the recesses of his mind, where it fed and bred, grew and boiled, until it had to erupt. It was killing him, eating away at him. No matter how often he pushed it back, it returned – sparked by a word, a sound, a smell, a memory returning to him in a quiet moment while eating his hay.

Now he stood at the back of his stable, mortified, trembling and shaking, alarmed with himself, upset about what he had done, uncertain about how I would react. I undid the bolt and went back in. Hector clamped his tail more tightly to his rump, shuffling his hooves further underneath him, his large, powerful quarters quivering and trembling. 'It's okay, Hector,' I said. 'I do understand. I don't know the best way to help you, but I do understand. You need to be free, don't you?'

He relaxed, perceptibly, half-closed his eyes, and stood less tensely, yet still the picture of shame, self-disgrace, and mortification. He was troubled and stuck, understanding himself so well, yet unable to find a solution. He didn't want to go out in the field and bite and punish the other horses, he didn't want to gallop around, screaming like a maniac, frightening Melissa and the others, he didn't want to fling his kind and sympathetic riders headlong into the middle of next week. So what options did he have? Only to hold on, and on, and on, until he could contain the violence no longer, then release a piece – a tiny, tiny piece – of what fed and festered within. But no sooner was that tiny piece free, than the beast within would breed and grow again.

Poor, poor Hector. I stood quietly again, wishing for something which would help, something that I could say or do. Suddenly, my mouth took on a life of its own. I took a deep breath and I roared:

'How *dare* you! How *dare* you!'

Not at Hector, but up at the stable roof, up into the sky, loud and clear and full of enraged meaning. Once again:

'How *dare* you do this!'

Expressing these words, the power was a force to be reckoned with. When a horse really speaks, it could lift the roof off an opera hall.

Although this may sound strange, speaking for horses is something that has happened to me a lot. I find it difficult to explain but it is as though I am some kind of voice recording device for them, and on their behalf. It is not so much that I choose what to say, or in what matter to express it; it is more that I am completely powerless to do anything else. I am usually, as was the case in this situation, very aware of my own mind, and often find myself thinking, 'Oh, here we go,' or 'This is a bit strong – how am I going to explain this one?', whilst my mouth is doing completely its own thing.

The words come with a force like a tornado, whipped up, as if by magic. My voice does not sound like my own, it sounds different with each horse. Hector felt and sounded like an old-fashioned boiler, spontaneously ignited by a timer switch; still and silent, then sparked into life, roaring upwards, full of impulsion and depth. As I say, I have no means of stopping these speeches when they come upon me, and they have, on occasions, got me into a great deal of trouble.

With Hector's voice, I felt that I had the power to lift the roof. I felt that I could yell up into the heavens and smash the clouds – burst the sun into a million shattered pieces, sending it firing in all directions across the bright blue sky. Such was the force of Hector's soul. It was not a mere expression of opinion, a small matter of a minor grudge, a lingering desire for someone, somewhere, to know how he felt. It was a passion; a living force, so raw, so blistered, so hurt and tender, yet so very powerful – so very strong and clear – and delivered with such projection.

At whom and why? I still do not know. I was not party to that information, but I pitied those people, the recipients. I pitied them greatly, for if that delivery, that profound message, reached them by way of the winds, the clouds, the cold, crisp air, I knew it would sear their very souls. They would not only hear it, they would feel it. They would know, and they would know the reason why. Sound carries, sound travels, and with it travels the message. The message was sent.

My mouth then returned to me. Having been given another voice, I was then given back my own; the fire was gone and I was myself again.

As had been the case whenever this had happened to me in the past, I automatically felt awkward. Here I was in a strange yard, having been invited to come and help, having been treated with open friendliness and warmth. And, in return, I had spent about 40 minutes doing what must have seemed like nothing, topped with about 30 seconds of bellowing like an enraged banshee at the rooftops. It is times like this when my conscience kicks in. *I know what has really happened, but does anyone else?* Perhaps I am destined for that fetching white jacket with sleeves which buckle up behind, after all. I hope not.

I left Hector then; his tail swinging softly by his hocks, his eyes wide and bright, his ears released from their stiff, upright position, now twitching gently from front to side. 'I hope you feel better now,' I murmured, as I stroked his neck gently.

I made my way back to the office, an old freight container that Melissa had found, supported and raised off the ground by railway sleepers, and tucked tightly against the stable block so as not to obstruct the entrance to the paddocks. This was where Melissa was waiting with bated breath, to hear what the problem was with her beloved Hector. I was very concerned that the office was so close to the stables. 'She must have heard me,' I thought. 'She probably thinks I'm some kind of maniac.'

Melissa greeted me with a cup of tea. 'How did it go?' Her eyes were eager but she had obviously heard some of my ranting, if not all of it. I paused before answering and saw her gaze lower to my crumpled scarf – soggy, pitted, and mottled with bits of half-chewed hay in a most decorative horse's teeth design. I too looked down, surveying the undeniable evidence for myself. I had not thought to look before, and now quickly began to rearrange my scarf, flicking off the chewed hay, and smoothing out the indentations, with as much of an offhand, 'oh, it's nothing' attitude as I could muster.

'Well,' I began, 'it seems that your Hector has been harbouring a bit of a grudge for some considerable length of time and, now and again, it seems to get on top of him a bit.' Melissa understood this only too well. I further went on to explain that he was very appreciative of her and all that she did for him, and that when he found himself unable to contain his need to express his emotions, he in no way intended to direct his feelings at her. Whenever he did, he always felt terribly ashamed of himself afterwards, but he really couldn't help himself at the time.

Melissa listened. She understood – completely and wholeheartedly. She sat with her gloved hands wrapped around her mug of tea, drawing on its warmth, and gently nodded her head by way of agreement. I finished my explanation by saying that I had 'had a little chat with him' and that she must just wait and see how he felt over the next few days.

A week later, back at the caravan, I sat chatting to Robert, catching up on all the news and recuperating from this latest trip which had lasted the best part of ten days. The phone rang and Robert answered, quickly passing the receiver to me.

It was Melissa. She told me that Hector was a reformed character. She was absolutely delighted. He seemed happier, friendlier, and so much more amenable – in fact, pleased to have her in the stable with him.

'I don't know what you said to him,' she laughed, 'but it seems to have worked!'

8

Sheep . . . and More Sheep

'*Yes!*' I shrieked, dancing twirls around the room. 'This is it! This is *it*! Oh, thank you, Universe!' I leapt up and down, clutching the handwritten message to my chest with both hands.

Robert and I had been looking, for quite some time now, for a yard complex with accommodation. Winter in the caravan and at Woodmore's was beginning to take its toll. Devon is not renowned for particularly cold temperatures, but frozen crusts on 'Mountainous Muckheaps', and icy gusts of sea wind bringing chiselled hailstones, seemed to sap our strength more and more. It was particularly hard on the horses; due to the change in wind direction, most of them were now directly facing the onslaught.

The caravan itself supported the subzero temperatures beautifully. The raindrops and condensation had turned to artistic frozen sculptures, and we would wake every morning to see new ice formations on the inner walls of the bedroom. Then we would rush to the small sitting-room to switch on the two-bar electric fire, fighting off our cocker spaniel for the closest position. In situations like this, concern for one's partner no longer exists, and it becomes a case of 'may the best man win'. The jostling between the three of us usually ended unsatisfactorily; red singed shins on myself, no eyebrows left on Snuffi, the spaniel, and poor Robert relegated to the kitchen to make the tea. By the time evening had come around, and we were fed and bathed, and Snuffi was finally satisfied with his body temperature, it would be time to go to bed and begin the cycle anew the following day.

We had looked at several potential yards but had not found any of them to be entirely suitable. They were either in the wrong location, without accommodation, with mobile accommodation (God forbid), affordable but too small, unaffordable and vast, or, quite simply, undesirable in every sense of the word. We were beginning to lose heart, but finally chose the soft option of advertising for ourselves. It was the reply to this advert that I now clasped to myself. At last, somewhere that sounded perfect.

It did indeed turn out too perfect – positively idyllic. There was one small hitch. The property had been on the market for quite some time, a few years, in fact, and would continue to be so, but we could lease it for six months if we wished. I did wish. Oh, how I wished. I did not regret the move from the farm to the caravan and Woodmore's, but we had not planned to stay there for as long as we had. We had hoped to find somewhere else before the winter set in, but this had not happened. Life has a habit of doing this. I often joke that it is because I am always so late; if I were not late, then things in our lives would not be late. I often threaten to put this theory to the test by changing, but funnily enough I haven't got round to this yet.

Other things had happened recently too – things that we had not planned. Fizz, Robert's collie, who so often took it upon herself to climb out of windows during the night, had found herself a boyfriend on one balmy, autumnal evening, and was now the proud mother of eight little collie puppies. We turned the conservatory-entrance of the caravan over to mother and pups; it was not possible to allow them into the main body of the caravan, but nor was there anywhere entirely suitable for them to live outside. So Robert built them a large wooden box and suspended an infra-red lamp to hang just above their hay-filled bed. It seemed to suit them admirably.

The only problem was when trying to come in via the front door. It was impossible to enter without being besieged by a flood of squeaky puppies, little pink tongues extruding and tails wagging frantically as they skidded across the lino floor. We took to flinging handfuls of puppy biscuits across the conservatory, in the opposite direction from the door which led into the caravan, otherwise a sea of puppies would escort one inside. Sometimes we were too slow and they did get into the caravan, whereupon they would run in all directions, up and down the corridor, and round and round the kitchen.

One of them seemed to have an absolute passion for making phone calls. He would make a beeline for the phone, seize hold of the cord, flip the receiver off its rest, then bounce up and down on the buttons, delighted with the beeping tones that he could hear. Most of the others only had eyes for Snuffi's ears and saw them as a play park. They would grab hold of them, then be swung round and dragged the length of the corridor and back as he made a desperate bid to shake them off. On top of all this, there was the trailing around behind them with rolls of toilet tissue when the sheer joy and excitement became too much!

I completed another series of trips while Robert made the necessary arrangements for our move. These included liaising with our bank who, it must be said, were tremendously supportive throughout – we had a lot to thank them for.

Arriving back home one mid-morning, I was greeted by Robert, cup of tea in one hand, keys to the hire van in the other. 'Here you go. The van is all loaded up. You drive this lot over and I'll stay here, see to the horses, and get the next load together and ready.'

I climbed into the van and was generously greeted by my dog Foxi and the Spaniel, Snuffi. Once the greetings had been largely exhausted – a process which took quite some time – and I had found most of the gear positions, I switched on the ignition and set off.

I had driven about two miles when I heard funny, little squeaky noises coming from the recesses of the tightly-packed Transit. I raised my eyebrows in alarm. 'Oh, God, he's packed a puppy by mistake.' The funny little squeaky noises became intermingled with funny little scratchy noises and, before long, the van echoed with a whole chorus of squeaky noises, and growly noises, and yelpy noises, and howly noises. And then came the smells – the smells that accompany such noises. Hardly surprising, really; one cannot expect only half a puppy to function.

Robert had done it to me again. There was no mistake. He just couldn't help it. Whenever there was difficult livestock to be moved, he always managed to see to it that I was the driver. This had happened to me on more than one occasion as I remembered only too well!

My mind swam back, back to the early days when I was renting the yard on the farm, and Robert's system of barter was at its height. He asked me one afternoon, in that charming way of his, sidling up to me, whether I could possibly do him a small favour, for which I would receive the bountiful payment of ten bales of his finest meadow hay. I suspect now that he knew that I would find it impossible to refuse such a tantalising offer. Pictures of my beloved horses with their mouths filled with sweet-smelling, soft, green hay, and sounds of contented munching, swirled around my mind.

'Sold. I'll do it,' I said. Then I realised that I'd forgotten to ask what 'it' was. I was so naïve back then.

Robert's face lit up. 'It's only a little job, you see, but a bit time-consuming. I'm a bit short-handed as John's at college, so if you could just drive the blue Escort van along to the vet's surgery at Dumplington – there are a couple of young rams in the back, booked in for "the snip".' He winced, visibly, as he said this and, foolishly, I put the request for my assistance down to male sensitivity. 'It won't take the vet two minutes, but you'll need to wait and bring them back again.'

Sounded simple enough to me. I took the directions, and my tobacco of course, down to where the blue van was parked outside the cattle yard. In I climbed and, on closing the door, glanced over my shoulder to cast my gaze over the two 'young' rams that were already loaded up. Obviously I was mistaken in my belief that young rams were about the size of a small collie dog. Robert had glossed over the fact that they were both more than adequately grown – and to a substantial size at that. Perhaps they were young of mind, or something. They were not what I had expected. Moreover, the distinct lack of partition between them and me seemed to have gone unnoticed. They could have both easily trampled their great bulks through the gap between the driver and passenger seats and taken over the driving at any given moment.

My attention was diverted by a knock on the window. It was Robert. I wound down the window as best I could with a handle that was coming adrift from the door. The window dropped a good six inches with a hefty 'thunk', and I found myself presented with a rolled-up magazine. As I accepted this gift, I listened in amazement and digested Robert's helpful advice: 'If you have any problems, distract them with this.' A cheery wave and he was gone.

'Distract who?' I thought, having visions of myself, bedecked with woolly ram on lap, frantically flailing the magazine out of the window to distract any unsuspecting pedestrians who might be endangered by our progress.

Not to be deterred and with the lure of those divine bales of sweet, juicy meadow hay calling to me, I set off slowly and gently. I didn't wish to alarm the rams any more than was necessary, especially considering the fact that they were not averse to delivering the odd butt or two when feeling threatened.

The drive to Dumplington was renowned for its beauty. From our farm there began a long winding rise to the highest village which sported the tiniest unmarked crossroads you would ever be likely to see on a main thoroughfare. It never seemed to matter from which direction one approached, it was always impossible to see at least two of the avenues leading off it. Luckily, I knew the road well enough.

From there the road began its long, swirling spiral downwards; swooping turns followed short, sharp hairpin bends, decorated on either side with the most glorious beech and chestnut trees. Strong, flexible boughs reached across the road and formed a canopy of green and gold as the summer sun shone rays of light through their leaves. The road then levelled out, snugly following the water meadows on the right which supported the River Exe, while keeping its line against the softening hillside on the left.

It was a truly beautiful drive, but I found myself denied the pleasures of this visual feast, not because of the rams, as one might suspect, but because of the van. Not only did the windows leap up and down in their sockets at will, but the gearbox had decided that second gear was of no benefit to anyone. To add to this, the driver's seat was largely unattached to the floor! I found myself zooming backwards, away from the steering wheel and the pedals, at the slightest inkling of a rise in the ground; all that stopped me was the bulk of the ram standing behind me as I crashed into his chest.

Hanging onto the steering wheel, perched precariously on the edge of this ejector seat, trying not to lose contact with the pedals, I searched desperately for second gear. It did not have one. Crunching and grinding to no avail, I had missed third gear, so all that was left was first. I ground down to first gear. The passenger side window expressed its approval by disappearing down into the door, leaving but a quarter of itself showing, and that tipped at an angle resembling the peak of an iceberg peeping out of the Arctic Sea.

My immediate concern was not for the fresh air that now swam around the van's interior – that was quite pleasant and largely cleared the choking exhaust fumes which had been seeping through the gap under the back doors. No, it was for travelling companion number two, who also appreciated the cooling breeze and was now reaching his nostrils towards the source of this summer air.

Fortunately, or unfortunately – I was unsure which – the road embarked upon one of its long, sweeping right-hand bends, and my seat responded accordingly, flipping me up against the driver's door. My surprise caused me to grasp the steering wheel too sharply and swerve violently across the road, sending both my woolly travelling companions over to the right to collide with each other. Now we were going downhill and, having momentarily forgotten that I was perched on the edge of the seat, I found myself slammed back to the floor and shot forwards, my knees banging against the steering column.

And so I continued my journey: flung backwards and forwards, and from side to side by the unattached seat; grinding from any gear one liked into any other gear that one didn't like; accompanied by windows that pleased themselves whether they opened or shut, and two very stunned rams who, I must say, were very little trouble at all. I spent most of the time apologising to them, telling them to hang on – a bend was coming up, or to look out, the seat was off again. We bounced off each other, or into each other, with little more than the odd bleat from them.

And this was how we did it, there and back. The homeward journey was a little more treacherous because of the grogginess of the rams, and the fact that most of the drive was uphill. But we made it.

As I pulled back into the yard, Robert emerged from the workshop. I climbed out of the van to hear him say, 'I'll bet that's the cheapest ten bales of hay you've ever earned!'

Having decided that I had learned my lesson after this enlightening experience, I was on my guard for the next few months. Whenever I was requested to do any 'little jobs', I made quite sure that I was in full possession of the facts. It wasn't so much that I wasn't prepared to help, more that I was *fully* prepared to help – if I needed shin pads, gauntlets, and a crash hat, then so be it. It was better to know in advance. I helped with many more things, often receiving bales of hay as payment, so it was well worth it.

On one particular morning, a golden opportunity came my way. Role reversal time. It was a quiet Sunday and most of the essential work had been done: horses fed, mucked out, and turned out, livestock checked, and yard tidied. Everyone had gone to their respective homes to enjoy their day of rest. I was the only one left on the farm. Pottering about my little cobbled yard, digging weeds out from between the cobbles with a hoofpick, I was distracted by a voice.

'Excuse me.' I looked up to see a gentleman looking over the gate. 'Do you have sheep?'

'Er, yes,' I replied. 'Not me personally, but the farm does.'

'Well, some of them might be yours – they've got out onto the main road.'

I thanked him kindly for letting me know, and said that I would find someone to do something about it. I thought he meant that four or five renegades had got out of the front meadow and were now lingering around the roadside, as was sometimes their wont. But he went on to explain that it was more like 200 of them, with definite ideas on a lengthy migration, since they were making their way, in no uncertain terms, along the road to pastures new, location unknown.

Alarm bells started to ring in my ears. There was no one on the farm except me, and there was no way that I could, or should, hang on till

Robert or anyone else arrived back. What I really needed was a dog. Foxi pricked up her ears and began to wag her tail frantically. 'No, I'm sorry, my love. Not you,' I told her, and put her in the tack room. She did not know how to work sheep, and it was better that she did not learn. The best dog, unfortunately, was not kept on the farm. He was brilliant but owing to his wonderful disposition, Adrian often took him home with him.

The only dog that was left was Gnasher. There was no mistaking his name – it was one he had all but given himself, since he could barely contain his delight in working sheep, and felt the need to sample their flavour at every given opportunity. He needed a careful eye kept on him when working, but, aside from this, he was a delightful dog.

He was black and white, quite a long-haired collie, with a face split half and half – one side black, the other white – giving him a strange, but very appealing, appearance. He was not a young dog any more, and had suffered a stroke a few years earlier which had left him with an undeniable tilt to his head, and a permanent smile – all of which added to his charm.

When I had first arrived on the farm, Gnasher had looked to be in quite a bad way, but having fallen madly in love with Foxi, and seizing every available opportunity to court her, his health had improved dramatically and he had gained a new lease of life, which was wonderful to see. He was no longer much used for work, although this, naturally, went against his personal choice. His owner was fiercely protective of him and could not bear the idea of him suffering more ill-health, so Gnasher was more or less retired.

I found him in his box at the back of the farm kitchen, snuggled up and asleep. I called him and he sprang to life, big fluffy tail wagging away. 'Gnasher,' I said, 'I've got some work for you to do.'

We set off down the drive, he following in true working collie style; trotting behind, then darting up to my left, then back and to my right, eyes glued to the ground the whole time and tail wagging in anticipation.

The sight that greeted me on the main road was one to behold. Before me I saw well over 200 sheep, all bleating, stretched out in broad formation, setting forth like a flock of geese on winter migration.

The leaders I could see, miles up the road, walking with fixed determination towards Devon. Somerset was obviously no longer the place to be. The others stretched left and right, filling the road. Some were in the ditch on the left while others were high up on the bank which bordered the road to my right. They were causing chaos. Cars on both sides of the road could go nowhere, cocooned as they were by sheep, bleating to the leaders and responding to the bleats that came back.

Gnasher's eyes were wide and bright. His big pink tongue extruded from his lopsided head and his fixed smile was now broader than ever. He sat in front of me, tail sweeping madly back and forth over the tarmac. He was awaiting instruction.

Surveying the mayhem before me once more, so that I might decide how best to direct my eager companion, I couldn't help but notice the keen anticipation of the occupants of the cars. They looked, mainly, to be tourists and were now rousing their squabbling children, and sitting up straight in their seats. They looked fascinated and intrigued, obviously hoping to witness a shining display straight from *One Man And His Dog*.

'Okay,' I thought. 'Here goes.' I looked at Gnasher, still positioned at my feet, ready and eager to obey. Then I remembered Robert's voice echoing through my mind: 'Gnasher's a really difficult dog to work, you know. He's been specifically trained by an old shepherd with such a strong Somerset accent and if you don't get the words just right, he goes haywire!'

Good job I'd remembered that. So, clearing my throat and adopting as much of a deep, male, Somerset tone as I could, I said, '*Gerrrt-on-bye dug!*', flung out my right arm and pointed to the right-hand flank of the flock.

Gnasher raised an eyebrow and cocked his tilted head even more to one side. His tail paused in its mad sweeping while he looked at me quizzically. He stayed exactly where he was, staring at me.

'Um, got that one wrong,' I thought. So I tried again – this time with more oomph. '*Gerrrt dug! Gerrrt-and-cum-bye-sheep!*' I had heard Gnasher's owner saying something very similar to him on one particular occasion.

Gnasher pinned both ears up this time, turned away from me, and eyed the sheep briefly. 'He's away!' I thought. But, no. He turned back to me, still smiling, and began wagging his tail with renewed vigour.

'Um, close that time. Maybe I've got my left and my right mixed up.' I was very aware by now of the tourists in their cars. Whatever must they be thinking? There I was, standing in the middle of the road, flinging hand signals and 'gerrrting' for all I was worth, and all to amuse a sheepdog who appeared totally unperturbed by the milling, ever-disappearing flock.

I tried, yet again; this time directing my semaphore to the left, and adding a few extra 'gherrrs' and 'urghhhs' for good measure.

Gnasher was delighted. No one had ever spent so much time amusing him with such gobbledygook. It was definitely worth being woken up for.

By now, my throat was completely raw. I had obviously not paid enough attention to Robert's explanations about working with a sheepdog. The tourists, by this stage, were beginning to realise what an incompetent I was. Then I had a clear thought – I never spoke to Gnasher like this. I talked to him a lot, especially when he came round to visit Foxi, but not like this. What on earth was I doing?

I took a deep breath, looked straight at Gnasher's still incredibly eager face, and said quietly, and with more than a touch of irony, 'Gnasher, go and get them.'

And he was away! Hallelujah!

He set off like a rocket. First up to the right, then over to the left, down the ditch sending hidden sheep scurrying out into the road, then spinning round the cars, directing sheep wherever he went. He set off after the leaders, caught up with them, and turned them round. Before long, all 230 sheep were under his control as he drove them back towards me.

Gnasher deserved a standing ovation. He was brilliant! Every now and then, he would pause to glance at me, wag his tail, and be off again. It was all I could do to contain myself from shouting words of encouragement such as 'Well done! Go for it!', but that would not have looked terribly professional. After all, earlier on I might just have been taking time out to instruct my dog in the utmost detail about the strategic plan I had devised for regaining order. Well, that's what I would have said, had any of the car's occupants called my bluff. They, like me, were obviously impressed.

As Gnasher brought the flock back down to the front meadows, Robert appeared on the quad-bike. His eyes were out on stalks. Could this possibly be me – and Gnasher – and all those sheep? He stopped the bike sideways across the road, just before the open gate, so as to direct the sheep back into their meadow.

'Gnasher,' I called, 'put them in there,' pointing to the open gateway.

'Wrrrooff!' came the reply. He wheeled the whole flock round, darting this way and that, giving a 'woof' here, a nudge there, and yes, unfortunately, the odd chomp here and there too but I pretended to take no notice of this. Soon the entire flock was returned to the meadow and the gate firmly latched behind them.

Thanking the tourists for their patience with a wave as they drove past, and giving Gnasher a big pat, I turned to Robert and said, 'It's easy when you know how!'

The puppies were, by now, quiet. They had largely exhausted themselves and, as puppies do, had fallen asleep. Robert, to his credit, had packed them in such a way as to keep them contained within their box, and the journey up the motorway to Gloucestershire went smoothly and easily.

Arriving at our new home, I was filled with the most delightful sense of joy. It was such a glorious place; a fifteenth-century moat house, complete with moat and a bridge to the front door. The house sat behind a neat yard complex of 12 stables, set in an offset U-shape. Coming through the entrance gates was almost unbelievable, like a dream come true. The complex also sported an office, tack room, feed room, rug room, small indoor arena, workshop, and six acres of grazing in post and railed paddocks.

The house came fully furnished and had the most beautiful garden overlooking the lush bottom paddocks. Around the yard were huge wooden tubs full of pansies, and the drive to the indoor arena lay beside an orchard of newly planted fruit trees. It was divine. I did so want my horses to have somewhere nice to live; some of them had not had the best of lives and I felt that they deserved this, perhaps more than any of us.

To top it all, we were inheriting two residents who went with the property – a large Muscovy duck, whom we christened Mrs Miggins and a very large, handsome tabby cat with white bib and paws, whom we named Harry-Cat.

They were both fantastically welcoming and friendly to our entire entourage, and by the time Fizz, the horses, and Geraldine, my goat, had arrived and been settled in, the menagerie was complete.

9

Remember Flower

Collecting animals has always been a passion of mine, originally beginning with the influence of my mother, although to this day it continues.

As a child, I would often pass a pet shop with my mother while out shopping. On one occasion, as we walked past, we spotted a very sad-looking gerbil in the window. Some days later the gerbil was still there, still looking sad. 'It's no good, I'm going to have to buy him,' said my mother, swinging sharp right into the pet shop doorway. Minutes later she emerged, armed with the gerbil in a box under one arm, and the necessities – food, cage, bedding – under the other. Home we went. Horace, as we named him, was soon safely ensconced in his new abode, and picked up very quickly, becoming friendly, cuddly, and active.

Another time, while buying fresh vegetables in the market in Münster, we came across a little black rabbit and a guinea-pig squashed together in a cage. It was a blisteringly hot day and the pair were stretched out panting with exhaustion from the heat of the sun and lack of water. 'Oh, that's terrible!' exclaimed my mother, promptly whipping deutschmarks from her purse and buying them.

I called the rabbit Aster and insisted that he should learn to showjump, which he did admirably well. The guinea-pig was named Panic-Pants. He delighted in having his chin scratched and would chunter his way around the lawn, completely ignoring the makeshift jumps.

Many more waifs followed: hedgehogs that the dogs brought in, needing lots of TLC after being terrorised by our hounds; two stray Alsatian puppies found dumped by the side of the road; a poodle puppy seen whining behind the glass of yet another pet shop window; a pony that no one else wanted, followed by another pony that other people wanted even less. And on the list went.

Nowadays, I try very hard to say no. I have to be very firm with myself because I am a complete pushover where these matters are concerned. Usually, I steel myself, grit my teeth and remind myself that I have no spare time or money for strays. On one particular occasion, however, my mouth declared, 'I'll have her!' I had intended to say, 'I'm sorry, it's not at all practical at the moment,' but my heart decided otherwise and I practically shouted, 'I'll have her!' and that was that.

The 'her' in question was a big chestnut thoroughbred mare, about 16.3hh with a white blaze and one white stocking behind. Hers was a tragic story. In training as a three-year-old, up in the north of England, she had shown little form, despite good breeding. Matters came to a head when she refused point-blank to go on the gallops, planting herself firmly and refusing to budge. It was rumoured that she was then tied by her neck to a Land Rover and dragged up the gallops, and this I believe to be true, since the damage to her neck was immense and irreparable. To accompany her war wounds she had contracted pedal ostitis, a painful condition of the hoof and, following the birth of several foals, she had also suffered bouts of laminitis, another severe foot condition.

She found her way to me via a series of different owners. When it had become obvious that she was not going to excel as a racehorse, she had spent several years as a brood mare. Eventually she had become barren, and ended up abandoned on a small stud farm as a bad debt, in lieu of her owners paying their bill. The stud subsequently sold her to recoup their losses. After she had produced a stillborn foal, the new owners eventually succeeded in breeding a live baby from her, followed by aborted twins, after which she became barren again. She was then left in a field for a total of eight years until she was given to Margaret Healy, a relative of her current owner, as a replacement for a recently lost hunter.

Margaret had every intention of hunting her new mare, but after eight years of little handling and no riding, the horse objected violently to the whole procedure. This behaviour seemed contrary to her nature as she had always been very sweet to catch and bring in from the field. Margaret subsequently turned to me for help. She asked me if I would get the horse working again, hopefully in time for the start of the hunting season. I agreed to take the mare for a two-week assessment period, after which I felt I would know better how to proceed.

I collected the mare from the stud which was next door to a dairy farm. I called her Flower, and she proved to be very kind, gentle, and easy to handle – until she was confronted with a bridle. Then she would break into a complete sweat. Shaking and trembling, she would paw the ground with her forelegs, first one then the other, smashing her joints hard on the stable door to the point at which she split them open. She seemed not to feel this, so overwhelmed was she by the presence of the bridle.

Deep down I was devastated on her behalf, but felt my responsibility to the business and her owner – bread and butter must come first. So I persevered, slowly and gently, letting her wear the bridle in the stable and bringing her a haynet at the same time, then leaving her alone in peace and quiet to eat. I would return a little later, groom her gently, then remove the bridle and leave her calmed. I hoped that this procedure would give her the space and time to readjust.

On reflection, most of my work to date with horses has brought with it an internal divide and moral dilemma. What I wanted to do back then with Flower was just hug her a lot but I had built a reputation which needed to be upheld. Also, I had to live; I had bills to pay and commitments to meet. When one's livelihood depends on others, one's obligations must always be placed first, and one's emotions second. I suspect that this holds true for the majority of people.

I continued to do my best for Flower, gradually reintroducing the saddle with a view to climbing on board. On the surface, throughout the entire process, she was very accepting and obliging, but the personality behind the façade puzzled me greatly.

She functioned to all extents and purposes just like every other horse; she pricked her ears and watched the goings-on in the yard, whickered for her food, made faces at the other horses as they passed her stable door, and appeared as intelligent and animated as all the others. Only she wasn't. All her external responses were automated; her behaviour was conditioned, a reflex to certain stimuli. In the same way that children leap up when the bell sounds to end a lesson – with no conscious thought – so Flower reacted to her environment. She was mindless. Her own decisions and choices were non-existent; she operated totally on auto-response.

Her reaction to the bridle said it all. In spite of our efforts to link the bridle with pleasurable things like eating, the moment she saw it she would begin to shake and sweat; the moment we removed it from her sight, she would stop and return to her haynet. She was devoid of a sense of self. I knew that it must still lie within her, but where? She couldn't possibly function like this. I was very upset at the state of her mind and emotions, but I still had her owner to contact and report to.

Decision time came, and at the end of the two-week assessment period, Margaret arrived at the yard, eager to find out how Flower was progressing. Margaret had a gregarious, fun-loving personality and was very much looking forward to the forthcoming hunting season on her new mount. I was not at all sure how best to explain things to her and felt very divided. I had a mental picture of myself, one foot on a jetty and the other on a boat as it pulled away, not sure which way to go. I did my best and explained as simply as I could.

I told Margaret that we had had Flower's feet checked, rebalanced, and appropriately shod by a renowned farrier. The vet who had ministered to her throughout her breeding period had been located, and had successfully treated her lameness problems, working in co-operation with the farrier. As far as he was able, he had given her the go-ahead, healthwise, and felt that she did have a future as a riding horse, providing her diet was attended to, and her fitness programme well thought-out and applied.

With the help and skill of these two professionals, it appeared, on the surface, that a dejected mare with a tragic past had been rescued and given a new lease of life. Margaret had, herself, been in touch with both vet and farrier, who had confirmed my report, which probably accounted for her cheerful mood as she stood listening to me.

Faced with Margaret's keen enthusiasm as she digested the news, I struggled with my conscience. It was no good; I couldn't help it – I had to speak for Flower. Taking a deep breath I explained that, while physically the mare might be all right, the biggest barrier to her well-being was her mental state. She had completely shut down and lived in a dream world – not fully comprehending life, just reacting to certain stimuli in a distressed manner.

I watched as the look of hope and delight slipped from Margaret's face to be replaced by one of despondency. I felt awful. I did not relish taking someone's dreams from them, but there was a choice to be made; what was best for the horse, or what was best for the owner. I chose the horse.

I explained further that, in time, Flower might very well make a riding horse, but there was no way that I could see this happening in time for the hunting season. Margaret was understanding but she maintained that her interests lay very firmly in the direction of hunting – and this season, not the next, or possibly even the one after that. If the mare was not up to it, then it would be unfair to expect her to cope. Which left her with a question. Who was going to want a

Having fun on the gallops riding Jelly Deal. He was an amazing three-year-old who everyone thought was hopeless but who came third in his first race. I'd love to know where he is now.

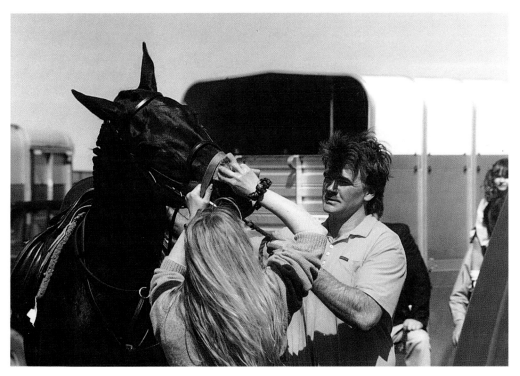

With Robert at a point-to-point.

Notes Again (commonly known as Herbie) was a favourite point-to-pointer until health problems occurred. We are now trying to overcome these problems.

Home Sweet Home! Our caravan home in Devon for 16 months.

Heaven! The Moat House. Definitely a change of scene.

Jackie working in the yard at the Moat House.

With Arnie on Emma's riding course.

Foxi – a true friend for the last 8 years. I acquired her from Battersea Dogs' Home when she was about 18 months old. She had been rescued after being dumped from a car.

Robert with Foxi's puppy, Dipper.

Showjumping with Foxi.

Geraldine is a much loved friend and a great character, who loves to join in whatever's going on. She came to me after being saved from the meat market by a friend of mine.

Snuffi is a pedigree cocker spaniel. I bought him from a friend in Somerset when he was a puppy and quite irresistible. He has always been good with the farm animals and has had many piglet and lamb friends.

Coffee, one of a group of four miniature Shetland ponies (known to us as the Munchkins) who came to us from Scotland whilst undergoing veterinary treatment. In the background is Harry.

large traumatised mare with a history of foot problems, and barren to boot?

She suggested that it might be better for Flower to be sent to the abattoir unless I could think of anyone who might want her. At this point, she looked at me enquiringly, her gaze clearly implying that I would make a perfect candidate for ownership.

This was the moment when my mouth took on a life of its own. The words leaped from my lips: 'I'll have her!'

Margaret, who was delighted to have solved her problem, recaptured her smile and delivered a hearty pat to Flower's neck before leaving the yard.

So that was that. I had another horse. I was delighted, and told Robert so when he came into the yard later on that day. Although he tried very hard to say the right things and look enthusiastic, there were obvious signs of strain in his eyes. I could almost read his thoughts, 'Another mouth to feed.'

But what of Flower? Where to start? Before leaving, Margaret had kindly volunteered information on Flower's sad and tragic past, complete with gory details of cruelty. The information hadn't helped much, it had merely left me feeling even more horrified, with a desire to seek revenge on these people for their injustices. I told myself that such thoughts wouldn't help anyone, least of all Flower herself, who still stood with that bemused, pleasant expression and empty eyes.

From thereon I gave Flower every opportunity to find pleasure in life again. I did go on to ride her when she was ready, and she was wonderful – soft, gentle and generous – but this was not what she wanted. I gave her the best I could in terms of emotional medicine: homoeopathy, aromatherapy, shiatsu. I would see small, short-lived improvements but, always, the same emptiness was present, or the distress.

To the external eye, she always looked well. Her coat shone and she maintained her gentle expression, but underneath was such a lot of pain. The vets could find nothing physically wrong with her, and yet every bone in her body ached and her nerves were raw. Great shock waves of pain would explode from her uterus through her pelvis and hips, run down her limbs and into her feet.

These pains were very real; tangible and physical. I knew that the cause of her pain was largely emotional, but I was at a loss to know how to get to the bottom of her problem. When her pain was at its worst I had remedies and medicine to hand which would ease the suffering, but it never entirely went away; never left for good. I tried everything to cure her but to no avail.

On one occasion, I resorted to getting cross with her, telling her, in no uncertain terms, that she was being stubborn in rejecting the very best of help, that she was only hurting herself – I cared about her deeply and wanted her to be happy and well again, to be free from her emotional torment, and to have peace and comfort in her life. She could have anything she wanted. If she wanted another foal, then she could have one – to keep – hang the expense. But if she persisted in clinging to something from her past, then she would only remain stuck in her own living hell.

My words had a profound effect on Flower. She began to sweat and shake. Trembling, she churned around in her stable, banging against the door and splitting her joints open. I burst into tears – huge wailing sobs that I couldn't control – so deep that I couldn't speak, couldn't breathe. My legs could hardly support my weight I was shaking so violently, and I could neither contain, nor stop, my sobbing.

This was Flower. This was her problem. Not a minor distress or trauma, but absolutely entrenching grief and shock – the most profound sense of devastation and utter despair – her mind completely devoid of any rational thought, but her emotions total and binding.

I have seen people, as perhaps everyone has, in a state of crisis when their emotions take over and become so whole and pure that they are scary to witness. Most of us express emotions on a daily basis but, when disaster strikes in catastrophic form, they take on a whole new dimension. Then they carry all the enormity of the force that nature exerts in a tidal wave, a raging forest fire, a hurricane – a force over which we have no control and little understanding. Pure emotion is perhaps the most powerful element within us all.

Maybe it was all of Flower's life force that I experienced in that moment, or maybe only part of it – I could not be sure. I only knew that the magnitude and the purity of it frightened me. Actors are paid enormous sums of money to portray convincingly feelings and emotions. They are nothing by comparison – a trickling brook against a raging torrent, a summer breeze against a tornado. Flower was the real thing – torment, grief, and shock – enough to burst flesh through skin, and tear nerves from tissue, reverberating with such force that her eyes could no longer see, her ears no longer hear, her lungs no longer expand, her blood no longer flow. This was her pain. This was her suffering. I had felt it, seen it and, moreover, for a few moments, had become it.

I didn't know the cause of Flower's torment, but the truth of it left me devastated and with an overwhelming sense of loneliness. I wanted to scoop her up and hold her in my arms, hold her close and take the pain away; just take away all of this pain. But, of course, this was impossible. She was a large horse and I was just a small person. I felt wiped out; totally wiped out, enfeebled, and inadequate. Yet still I clung to the hope that I would find a solution.

One lovely, sunny afternoon in summer I went to see Flower in the orchard. I had just come back from travelling a great deal, and was looking forward to a few days' peace at home with my own horses. She had been on my mind a lot.

She was currently undergoing treatment from our vet, as the trauma had started to manifest itself into a more serious physical condition. All the major nerves throughout her body felt white hot, like those of a tooth suddenly exposed to the air by the dentist's drill. I desperately wanted to do something for her, even a little personal something.

We all knew that her time had nearly come, and we were happy with that decision, although her passing would leave us with a sense of great loss. She lived as free a life as we were able to provide for her. Her stable was kept full of soft, fluffy bedding, its door always open so she could come and go at will, as was the gate to the orchard. She was even allowed to eat the pansies from the flower tubs as she wandered around the yard. Our office was also in the yard and she would often stick her head in, rifling through the box of teabags on the table, or playing with the cups on the draining board.

That afternoon, I found her under the fruit trees in the orchard, mooching around and grazing in the shade. I sat down in the long grass beside the gate and watched her, feeling tears well in my eyes and a lump form in my throat. 'Flower, what would be your wish – the greatest wish you could possibly have?' It wasn't an audible question; almost more of a wish of my own. A desperate last hope, perhaps.

As she swished her tail in the warm sunshine, I saw a small glimmer of softness enter her eyes. She glanced at me, not pausing from her grazing but pricking her ears towards me. Yes, it was there, a tiny hint of warmth; a small suggestion of a conscious thought, breaking through her protective dream world. 'What Flower? What is it?'

Sitting there in the grass I felt myself suddenly besieged. A thunderbolt of emotions, sights, smells, and sounds, stormed through my body and my mind; wave after wave of heart-wrenching sensations. Grief. Grief and despair.

And the noise . . . the noise . . . not loud, but filling my whole being

– the stricken sound of little four- and five-month-old foals, screaming their little lungs out. Now bellowing and hollering – this time from calves, wave after wave of little black and white calves, their pink mouths open, bawling and bellowing. Now the foals again – shrill, terrified, elongated calls, interspersed with the tormented answers of the mares. And cows – louder now – nearly drowning out the cries of their little ones.

These sounds I had heard before, and they had always distressed me greatly. In our world, we hear weanlings and we may do our best to comfort them, hoping with a twinge of pity or anguish that the sound doesn't continue for too long. We wonder, briefly, whether the separation of mother and baby is fair, or whether it is for the best. Fleeting thoughts.

But this was from a whole new perspective. This was the sounds explained, given clarity, and truth, and meaning. The message delivered with emotion – the most powerful of all communication.

It was over as quickly as it had started. I sat stunned, in my own state of trauma, looking at Flower. Her eyes were soft and shielded, hurt but hopeful.

I understood. This was her world. This was why she had shut herself away. Mere words are inadequate to describe the insight into the emotions that Flower bestowed upon me that day. Nor can I begin to describe the profound effect such experiences had undoubtedly had upon her own life, and the lives of her foals. Not only had she had to contend with her own personal losses, but she had also withstood eight years of empathising with the cows from the neighbouring dairy herd – their torment no greater or lesser than hers, and just as profound.

Her mind must have reached the point where it could no longer cope; the stillborn foal and the aborted twins contributing to her need to escape, to shut down and close herself away from the torment – a desire to live in a dream world where time passes without meaning or emphasis – a desire to wrap a protective cloak around her heart and tie it tight. To stay shut away, safe from life.

'You have heard their screams.' This floated through my mind with the softness of a breeze, with the lightness of a butterfly. This was Flower. 'Now you have *felt* their screams.'

So true. I cannot convey to you the horror of what I experienced, but the truth of it would crack open the hardest of hearts and reduce it to rubble. I endured it, felt its impact, indeed, became it, for but a brief moment. Flower *lived* it – time, after time, after time.

I can only relate to you Flower's story. But I can ask of you something much more.

If you ever find yourself caught in the middle of a storm, a raging tempest of monumental violence which causes you to clasp your ears against the crashing thunderclaps, and flinch from the lightning snaking viciously to earth around you – when you feel the trees shake, whipped back and forth in frenzy; when you feel the ground tremble from the vibration of the energy in the charged air; when you feel the raw and absolute power of uncaring elements, that have no respect for authority, wealth, position – or you; when you can only wait and pray for it to end – feeling small, insignificant, abandoned, frightened, helpless . . .

Remember Flower.

10

A Question of Understanding

How much do animals understand? This is a question that so many people have asked me. I used to answer without a qualm, 'Oh, everything'. Then I began to realise, over the course of time, that this was not necessarily the case. First and foremost, much seems to depend on how much they want to understand, and secondly, and equally important, on how clear we make ourselves. Some animals are, as we might describe, more 'intelligent' than others. But that is such a debatable statement. What is intelligence?

During the course of my visits, I encountered a vast array of human perceptions regarding animal intelligence, and also discovered that my own perception of that intelligence was sometimes a million miles away from that of my clients.

One lady whom I remember had an elderly horse that she had owned since her youth. She, herself, was a very strong character and held very strong opinions. She was dying to talk to her horse, but her assumption soon became apparent; she was convinced that he would return the parlance with witticisms and anecdotes – enough to reduce everyone to fits of hysterical laughter, and stun everybody's minds with his blinding intelligence. She had gathered together a group of friends for this very purpose.

I was somewhat perturbed by this from the outset. It is always very difficult for me to ask open and objective questions of an animal when I find myself faced with a predetermined, humanised opinion of them. The difficulty is such that, if I am not careful, it can colour the manner in which I ask my questions.

For example, if one wished to know the answer to a simple question, such as 'Why do you stamp your feet on the ground?', one would need to genuinely want to know the answer, without disapproval or assumption.

If one were to ask this question coloured with an undertone of disapproval, then it would become completely different. The whole meaning would change, and one might just as well say, ' I don't see any need for you to stamp your feet on the ground like that.' That which was a question, is now a statement; one no longer has a question, and consequently, there can be no answer.

If, on the other hand, the same question was asked with a preconceived assumption – based on the fact that one had witnessed the animal repeating this behaviour over a period of time, and one believed it to be in connection with food – then one would be asking a leading question. Now one might just as well ask, 'You stamp your feet on the ground because you want your food, don't you?' The whole emphasis of the question has changed again, and the answer can only be 'yes', or 'no'. 'Yes' reinforces one's assumption, while 'no' goes against it – and one still does not have the answer.

In cases such as this, when the answer is 'no', the client immediately becomes very suspicious, and I find myself in the position of having to explain, in great detail, why they have received an unsatisfactory answer. The client is then required to drop all assumptions as regards this question – and all subsequent questions they may wish to ask.

I am sure that this must sound terribly complicated and – believe me – it is! It was with the aforementioned lady.

She wanted me to ask her horse several of what I call 'loaded questions'. Each one had an undercurrent. Her horse understood the undercurrent better than the questions, and so the conversation went something along the following lines:

'Ask him how he gets out of the stable'; a statement if ever there was one – the real meaning being, 'He's so clever, the way in which he gets out of the stable.'

Reply from the horse: 'She likes me to do it'; meaning, 'I hope that's the answer she wanted.'

'Yes, but ask him how.'

So I asked him how. 'She means tell her exactly what you do to get out of the stable.' This question I asked telepathically.

Horse looked momentarily confused and I felt his confusion. 'Why are you confused?' I asked in my head.

Horse's reply: 'She wants me to do something for her friends.'

'Oh, okay. What does she want you to do?' Again in my head.

'I don't know, but I feel that she does.'

'Oh, dear me,' I thought. Never mind. I tried again.

'Can you tell me how you get out of the stable?'

'Yes. I undo the door.'

There. I had it. I turned to the lady and said, 'He opens the bolt on the door.'

She beamed with delight. 'Oh, he's so naughty'; meaning, 'He's so clever.'

Need I go on. By the time I had finished, my brain was addled. I felt quite light-headed and muddled – as did the horse. It was like being under the spotlight on *Mastermind*, with a series of complex questions being flung at you, all with different meanings.

Having spent so much time now conversing with other people's animals, I have become very attuned to any undercurrents lurking behind the questions that I am requested to ask. Although most of my clients have been fantastic, there were definitely some who found my abilities amusing, and who felt the need to play games.

Since I am normally very mild-mannered, I was able to cope with these instances fairly well, but I did find it very trying, and it saddened me that these people thought so little of their respective animals that they would not grant them the opportunity to speak openly, or allow themselves to listen honestly. Usually I tell people in situations like this that they are shooting themselves in the foot, and if that is what they wish to do, then so be it.

Some clients, however, were more honestly sceptical than others. One lady told me, quite clearly, as soon as I arrived on the premises, 'I'm extremely sceptical about this sort of thing, but if you prove yourself, then I'll sing your praises.'

I felt this to be fair enough, and said as much in reply. We went to her horse, and she asked a series of questions and got her replies – clear, concise and accurate. I don't think that she was aware of the fact that she was, herself, brutally honest – in spite of her scepticism. It was her honesty that won the day, her horse being brutally honest in return.

I had to laugh when, some weeks later, word having spread, a new client rang on a referral basis from the previous lady.

'Mrs X tells me that you're marvellous,' she said, 'I'd like you to come and see four horses at my yard. There is possibly a fifth, but Mrs X advises against it for that particular owner, as she says you are definitely not for the faint-hearted.'

Some of the people that I visited were quite obviously afraid that I was reading their minds to gain information, as opposed to communicating directly with their horses. But I was not. Many of them sheepishly admitted to me afterwards, that they had gone to great lengths to think all manner of confusing things to prevent me from doing this – such as concentrating intently on the contents of their briefcase!

When I first began to travel, I hadn't the vaguest notion of all that I would encounter on my visits. Nor was I aware of the complexities that would be required from me, in order to carry out my consultations. My intention had been solely to help animals in any way that I could, but I had not realised the magnitude of the work involved. As a result, I learned a great deal about tact, diplomacy, and whom to trust. But on the whole, most of the visits turned out to be enjoyable experiences for me, and some went on to become treasured memories. I hope that these are equally treasured by the animals and their owners alike.

The memory of one dog in particular is most pleasurable. I had been called in to see a horse belonging to a young woman who worked on a farm. After finishing my consultation, I found myself chatting to the chap who owned the farm. He turned out to be passionate about his dogs, of which there were many – working collies and Alsatians. He knew each one of them by heart – exactly what they liked, and exactly what they didn't like – and he understood their personalities inside-out. He spoke about them with love and pride, each in turn, and each for different reasons. And they, themselves, were clearly devoted to him.

The conversation turned to a little collie dog that was chained up at the back of the straw barn. The farmer spoke with sadness, explaining that the dog needed an operation on his leg and was booked in for surgery the following week. As he spoke, the little dog tucked himself up tighter into a ball, bewildered eyes looking up, then back down again as he heard his name being mentioned. Enormous worry was written all over his furrowed brow.

I asked what the problem was and the farmer explained that Charlie had been unable to put his leg to the ground for some weeks now. It was obviously terribly sore and uncomfortable; each time the vet had examined it, Charlie had cried out in pain and pulled away. They had decided to operate on the tendons to see if that would help.

Charlie was clearly worried and afraid, so I asked whether I could take a look. The farmer was only too delighted, but warned that he could be a little untrustworthy with people that he didn't know.

Too late – I was in there like a shot. Kneeling down beside the little dog, I said, 'Can I have a look at your leg then, Charlie?'

Charlie looked alarmed and worried. He drew his leg up tighter to his body and became defensive. At this point the farmer came over to us and said, 'I'll let him off his chain and then you can see'.

He did this and Charlie stottered out from the barn, a sorry-looking sight indeed, hopping along with one hind leg tucked high up underneath him.

'There you are, you see,' said the farmer, his voice filled with sorrow. 'Looks bad, doesn't it?'

I'm not sure why, but I felt intuitively that something was very amiss here. Somehow, the leg seemed to be all right, even though it was held, tucked up, at a strange angle.

I knelt down in front of Charlie, held his head in my hands and asked, 'Charlie, what is the matter with your leg?' This is the point at which one has to be completely open and drop all assumptions.

Charlie's eyes darted this way and that. Then – like a whisper – it came. 'They are going to chop it off.'

Normally, in situations like this, I am terribly sympathetic, but this time I could only just hang on to my laughter. I was not laughing at the dog, merely at the reality. Every time his leg had been examined, he had become unmistakably aware of the low murmurings of the farmer and the vet. 'Mmm, it's not good, is it?' They would both observe the limb and shake their heads slowly from side to side. 'Doesn't look good, does it?' Then they would walk away and talk almost inaudibly.

Charlie had listened, understanding the odd word here and there, but only in association with farming. Words such as 'joint' had specific meaning for him, as did 'tender' – presumably close to 'tendon' – and 'cut'. The vet, of course, meant big trouble. As was the case with most farmers, the vet was only called when he was really needed – the farming profession, itself, requiring a sound management of all ailments and injuries. Vets, therefore, meant serious business.

Charlie, using his intelligence, had put these odd words together, and had convinced himself that he was about to become an amputee!

I pulled his head into my chest, rubbing his ears with delight. 'Oh, Charlie, no! That's not what they're going to do!'

The farmer, looking on, asked 'What? What is it?'

I told him. 'Charlie has been listening to you and the vet. He thinks you're going to chop his leg off as it's no good any more. He likes his leg and wants to keep it.' By now I was laughing. Charlie understood that I wasn't laughing at him, just with sheer pleasure at his fantastic ability to make word associations, and also because, what had looked so very grim, was actually so easy to solve.

Charlie laughed too. He ran round in circles, barking with joy. The poor leg, which had seemed to be no good any more, was now back to its normal position, in full use and only the odd limp or two to be seen. It was a far cry from the useless appendage which had been there but a moment earlier.

'My God!' exclaimed the farmer. 'Will you look at that!' He scratched his balding head in disbelief and slapped his checked cap against his thigh in the way that farmers do. Then everyone started to laugh. Watching Charlie jumping with glee on all four legs was a wonderful sight.

'What makes him limp like that?' asked one of the farm hands, also extremely concerned for Charlie. I didn't know so I said I'd ask.

Calling Charlie to me, I asked him why he had begun limping in the first place. In response, Charlie flopped down onto his back and stretched his head flat back against the ground, front paws tucked together and hind legs splayed; his undercarriage exposed for all the world to see, as if basking in the sun.

'Oh, you daft dog!' said someone.

I knew that this dog was far from daft, so I asked him what he was trying to show us. Then it dawned on me – it was quite obvious, really.

'It's his you-know-whatsit!' I exclaimed.

We all peered intently, and on close examination, could see that it was a bit swollen and sore-looking. Giving him a prod around this area, the farmer's wife found a very tender spot. When she touched it, Charlie squeaked, a little high-pitched yelp. No mistaking that – that meant 'ouch!'.

Charlie was now up and off again, bouncing around and yapping with delight. One could almost imagine him singing, 'They've-found-it, they've-found-it', in child-like rhyme.

Everyone was thrilled, and tea with chocolate cake became very much the order of the day.

Sitting in the lovely farmhouse kitchen, drinking tea, eating cake, and answering as many questions as I could, was a thoroughly enjoyable experience. They were all lovely people – passionate about their animals, and greatly concerned for their well-being. It was a shame to have to leave, but time was getting on, and I had quite a drive ahead of me.

As I was about to say my goodbyes, the farmer's wife, Mary, turned to me and said, 'Actually, there is one thing I would like to know. I found my cat dead outside a few weeks ago. It hadn't been mauled or anything, but it was definitely a bit scraped and ruffled-up. I know that it wasn't Lucy or Rex, and I can't imagine it to have been Cider or Percy. I think it was either Shep or Charlie – and to be quite honest, it's more likely to have been Charlie. Would you ask him for me?'

'I'll ask,' I replied, 'but with matters like this, he might not tell me.' She was obviously upset about her cat, as one might well imagine. Bearing in mind Charlie's intelligence, I realised that this would definitely require tactful handling.

Charlie was sitting outside the kitchen door listening, true to form. As soon as we came out, he looked decidedly sheepish, guilt written right across his eyes. I had to keep my focus, though – it was imperative that I saw him as innocent until proven guilty.

The entire entourage from the kitchen stood over him, looking down and awaiting a full confession. This proved too much even for Charlie, and he slunk to the floor, grovelling and sliding along on his belly, nose between his paws.

'I knew it!' exclaimed Mary. 'I knew it was him!' She was not motivated to find the culprit out of a need to punish, more to satisfy her own mind and lay her suspicions to rest once and for all.

I asked everyone to leave, to give myself and Charlie the space we needed. Everyone dutifully obliged and we were left on our own.

'I don't think that they are still cross with you Charlie but they would like to know. Your lady found her cat dead and was very upset. She would just like to know whether you had anything to do with it.'

Question asked, I waited for a reply. I honestly wasn't sure whether he would answer at all, for there is one thing that I must say about animals – they never lie. If in doubt, they say nothing. I expected to draw a complete blank with Charlie but I was proved wrong.

Charlie gave. He gave me all the information, and in the greatest detail. How he'd liked the cat, thought it such fun as he'd chased it this way and that – underneath that car, around that flower bed, and up that tree. He went to great lengths to show me each location, and each fixed structure, around the farmyard where the cat had been chased. He further went on to explain how one day, during their usual escapade, the cat had suddenly decided to lie down – right over there – and not get up again. And that was that – game over – it just would not get up and play any more.

I immediately surmised that said cat had had a heart attack. I said as much to Charlie and told him not to worry, these things happened and it was okay. He perked up and wagged his tail.

I then called the others back and repeated everything that Charlie had told me. When I had finished, Sally, whose horse I had come to see, said, 'Wow! That's amazing. That's the exact spot where we found Tiddles.'

I looked at Mary who appeared a little bemused. 'Yes,' she said. 'That's exactly the spot where we found Tiddles. But I wasn't asking about Tiddles – that happened about five years ago! I was talking about Suki, and that happened only about a month ago! And he knows it, the little so-and-so! Where is he?'

We all looked round for Charlie. None of us had noticed the fact that he had disappeared. He had slunk off, very quietly, to sit behind Jacob, one of the farm workers. Making himself as invisible as possible, he now sat tight up against the back of Jacob's legs, in a trim upright position, tail curled around his paws. The expression on his face said it all – 'Oops!'

I laughed most of the way back to the motorway thanks to Charlie. He'd made my day. When one meets such an animal, everything gets put into perspective. What is intelligence anyway? To me, they are all intelligent, but their intelligence differs greatly, and it is always in keeping with their species.

Motorway driving allows for excellent reminiscing and thinking time, although I am sure that the police and motoring lobbyists would be shocked and horrified by such a confession. I am certainly not the only one who does this. Driving along, all one seems to encounter in the main are blank-faced people, operating their cars in an auto-pilot mind state. I often wonder whether they are thinking such bizarre things as I am.

On this occasion, I began to think of cows. Yes, cows. They too are the most wonderful creatures: kind, sympathetic, and full of their own intelligence. I've no doubt that those of you who spend a great deal of time around them, will not have failed to notice their amazing social and family philosophy.

Up until meeting Robert, I had had little to do with cows, although I had always liked them as a child, particularly calves. Perhaps one can put this down to their prettiness. They have the most wonderfully shaped faces; wide and sculptured with fabulous cheekbones, long-lashed eyes, and beautifully curved indentations sloping down to a shapely nose. Complete with those inquisitive ears, they are not too far removed from a deer. Robert was passionate about his cows and it was on the farm that I had my first opportunity to really understand them better.

It was calving time, which follows lambing time. While everyone was all but exhausted by the never-ending flood of new woolly lambs, there was just enough time to rebuild reserves of strength before the arrival of the calves.

Since Mother Nature will always have her way, there was a degree of mortality involved. This, of course, was a fact of life, and although any loss was always sad, life had to go on; the focus being to do what was best for the surviving mother or calf, whichever was the case.

This time around it was two mothers who passed on to the great, green pastures in the sky. Neither was young, and each had produced a beautiful calf, which they had nursed and cherished until about a month old. Robert felt very strongly that since both the 'old dames', as he called them, had been great friends for many years, it was largely the parting of the first, from staggers, which had taken the other.

But what of their calves? Farm policy was to take the orphans and sell them to the dealer. Robert had used this dealer, on occasion, to purchase orphaned calves from other herds within the county, and present them to childless mothers for approval and subsequent adoption. This had always worked extremely well, and many a happy, wholesome relationship had been born in this way.

Robert made the phone call, saddened to lose the two mothers and even more saddened to be sending away two of his babies. After all, it was he who had been with the cows when the calves had been born, he who had soothed, aided, and calmed them in the middle of the night; it was he who had helped to dry off the gangly new-borns, and he who had taken them to the pastures with their mothers and watched them frolic for the first time.

Robert used to describe the new calves as being like little dodgem cars as they galloped around testing their legs, for they would often hold their tails straight up as they bucked and gambolled into each other, all wide-eyed and snorting. The 'old dames' would often decide to join in. They would canter and buck, dropping their heads to the ground and shaking them from side to side. It was wonderful to see.

Phone call made, it was now time to bring in the herd and pick out the orphans. Robert finished his cup of tea and, without another word, took his dog and went to meet Adrian in the yard. From here they would take the quad-bike and drive up to the far end of the farm where the cows and calves were grazing the spring meadows.

Before very long, I heard them return and put the herd in the cattle yard at the back of our little house. I was doing my paperwork and, having a natural inclination to shy away from matters such as these, buried my head deeper into my figures, and closed my ears to the noises coming from outside.

Cows have a very powerful voice; I cannot, for the life of me, understand the person who first described the noise that they make as 'moo'. Their voice begins on a deep, low, strong resonance, gaining in power and tone as the sound is projected. They always finish on a louder, stronger note than that with which they started. Perhaps it is impossible to find the right match of letters to give true clarity and meaning to the sounds that they make and so for the time being, 'moo' must suffice.

I was not fully conscious of the time, but a great deal seemed to have elapsed before Robert came bursting through the door. He was hot, sweaty, dirty, dishevelled – and upset. In that typical male way of his, he stomped and crashed about as a cover for his real feelings. Slamming the door behind him, slapping his gloves down on the table, and ripping open his jacket, he stormed, 'Come and sort these flaming cows out!'

'Why?' I asked, almost quaking in my slippers. Robert in a mood is not a pretty sight; it brings out the Scotsman in him more than ever, and he also sports what we jokingly refer to as 'The R. Mackay Death-Glare'. This is no joke – one look is enough to disintegrate one's innards for good.

He was a little short of this right now, but not too far off. Not particularly wishing him to move further into the realms of 'Hairy Highlander' territory, I offered him a cup of coffee. He accepted, and agreed that it would be a good idea to take some time out and let matters calm down. I made hot drinks all round since Adrian had also come in to rest his weary muscles for ten minutes or so.

Adrian was always very, very cheerful, not forcibly so, but just that way inclined. No matter what the time of day, whatever he was doing, Adrian usually had a smile on his face, and could drum up a laugh or two.

He now explained, in his sunny way, that it was mayhem outside. The cows were behaving most oddly. Each time he and Robert felt that they had identified one of the orphans, and attempted to move it into the adjoining pen, one or other of the 'old dames' would rush forward to claim it for her own. Believing that they had made a mistake, they would turn their attention to another calf standing alone. Moving this next towards the second pen would bring about a similar response from another of the cows. And so this cycle had gone on – for nearly two hours.

Adrian and Robert felt that they had, undoubtedly, been around the whole herd twice. They were now at a complete loss as to how they were going to isolate either of the orphaned calves. This had never happened before, and when one is required to suppress all personal feelings in order to complete a job, such complications do not make life easy.

The atmosphere being somewhat calmer, Robert said that he wanted me to find the orphans for him. This was very difficult for him at the time; although he was very aware of my communication skills, and had not the slightest doubt about them when it came to horses, he was not altogether sure of my accuracy where livestock were concerned. In fact, he told me that he was very sceptical, but would wait and see before making up his mind.

At the time, I remember feeling mortally wounded, although in true Mackay style I did not allow this to show. I realise now, though, that the very nature of my ability placed Robert's occupation under threat. He loved his cows and could manage them with great concern, provided that he kept them in their place as cows – animals without too much emotion or feeling. He credited them with enough emotion to allow himself to admire them, but not enough to allow himself to get close to them. Should he ever get too close, he would not be able to manage them with the priority being, first and foremost, on management. If he allowed his personal feelings full rein, then his perspective would have to change. So, he prided himself on being a good manager – which he was – and tried very hard not to notice too much personality in his beloved cows.

The three of us went outside and entered the cattle yard. The herd had settled down and were munching their haylage. On our arrival, they all stopped their munching and stared at us, as if of one mind – completely together and in harmony.

The matriarch of the herd took two small steps forward to make herself known. It was to her that I addressed myself. Very aware that my emotionally sensitive and sceptical husband was watching me, I decided not to do this one out aloud.

I looked at the lead cow. On reflection, this was probably not the most polite way to greet her, but I wasn't overly familiar with bovine protocol back then. In fact, I was quite ignorant of it, or I wouldn't have asked the questions that I did.

'Is that one of the orphan calves?' I asked quietly in my head, gesturing with my eyebrows at a fawn-coloured calf standing to her left. Adrian had strongly expressed that, in his opinion, it was, which was why I was asking specifically about this one.

What I received by way of response was not exactly a reply; it was more a sensation of 'absolutely not'. No words with it, or pictures, no soft gliding sensations wrapped in emotion – just a stiffening from within, as if my gut had gone into a knot. It was not a knot of dread; it was a knot of determination – much as I would have felt had I encountered something of which I strongly disapproved. I took it to mean 'no', in no uncertain terms.

I told Robert and Adrian that this was not the one. Robert then pointed towards another – one that he suspected, and felt quite strongly to be an orphan.

So I began again, addressing the matriarch. 'Is that one of the orphan calves?'

I received the same sensation – a definite knot and hardening in my gut. Again, no fear or trepidation – just stalwart disapproval.

This must be how cows communicate, I thought at the time. It felt very different from horses, and was a whole new experience. I was half inclined to tell Robert and Adrian how interesting this was for me, but on seeing their frowning faces, decided against it – it was apparently not the time or the place. They had both been convinced of their accuracy, and being proved wrong was, seemingly, no credit to their herdsmanship.

The three of us stood there, faced by the attentive, immobile herd; Robert and Adrian casting their eyes over each calf in turn. We decided that it would be easier to narrow down the numbers; if not, we might well still be standing here in the morning.

We, or I should say, they – for I knew none of the cows – began to rule out the ones which, for certain, belonged. While they were doing this, I felt it would be easier for me to look to the calves, rather than deal with the matriarch or any of the other cows.

Glancing around, I just caught a glimpse of a little calf peeping out at me from between the front legs of one of the cows. As soon as I looked at it, I knew it was one. But no sooner had I spotted it, than it darted its head away to one side, so that I could no longer see its eyes, or it, mine. That was one!

'There's one!' I called to Robert excitedly. 'There! Right there in the middle!' Both Robert and Adrian looked, peering and straining to get a clearer view of the calf.

No sooner had I said this than my gut went into spasm. A most peculiar feeling, similar to before only much stronger, as though a hand were around my innards – not squeezing hard, but holding firmly – very much there.

Straightaway, I realised that I had done wrong. Yes, I had found one of the orphans but, oh boy, had I upset the matriarch. It all happened so quickly, and within me. As quickly as I recognised the injustice I had done the herd leader, my mind lit up with the solution. Again, not a picture or words, but a spontaneous total understanding, as if a light switch had been flicked on inside my head, and was now illuminating my mind with its fluorescent bulb.

I turned to Robert and Adrian and spoke very quickly, not thinking before the words came.

'The herd wants to keep them. They will all look after them and take turns to feed them. They made this promise to their departed mothers and they want to honour it.'

Poor Robert. The colour all but drained from his face. I'm sure all sorts of thoughts swam round his head at the time, but the worst problem for him was farm policy. How on earth was he going to get around this one? He knew, only too well, that his employer would expect the orphans to have been sold, and would ask specifically about them at the next farm management meeting.

But what about the cows? He *knew* now, so there was no going back. He had a choice to make – almost a no-win decision. Could he place his profession and respect for his employer over the remarkable family loyalty and love within this herd of cattle for which he cared so much?

He pondered for a moment, chewing his lip. Adrian looked relieved that the decision was not his to make, and began an investigation of the treads on his wellington boots. The cows remained still, just as they had been – as of one mind, and in total unison.

An age seemed to pass with nothing said. Then Robert spoke hurriedly, the rush of words falling from his mouth as if there was a danger of them being eaten and replaced with others.

'I'll give them one month. But if any of the calves loses condition at all, then that's it!'

He then turned on his heels and left the pen. He would not change his mind now, and he would, indeed, give them that one month. He meant it, and the cows knew.

The herd was taken back to their sweet meadow pasture and watched very carefully by Robert throughout the following month.

He never did distinguish the orphan calves from the others. They all grew together, not one losing condition, not one out-growing another.

And so they all stayed together: as of one mind, and in total harmony.

11

Beware Hippos!

I consider myself most fortunate to have had my father-in-law living in Kenya. It is the place of Robert's birth, and although the rest of the family had returned on many occasions to visit, Robert had not. His father had come to England to work when Robert was still a child, and only in later years had he returned to Africa.

Robert made the arrangements for us to go and visit well in advance. We both felt that it was an absolute must, and if we did not book so far in advance we would probably get waylaid by one thing or another. It is not usual for us to take holidays since we are both busy and embroiled in our work. The only two that we have had, have both been quite exotic: the first to the Cayman Islands, where my father had taken up the post of Medical Officer to the Islands; and the second to Africa. Had it not been for our respective parents residing in these wonderful places, our meagre budget would never have come close.

I found it very difficult to leave my horses and felt guilty right up to the moment when we boarded the plane. I do this all the time – even when I am travelling but two counties away on my visits, I feel guilty to be leaving them.

Kenya turned out to be fantastic, and Robert's father, aware of my addiction to horses, had made some arrangements for me to ride, lest I should suffer withdrawal symptoms.

He had some friends who lived on the other side of the lake, who owned racehorses. The wife, who was called Patricia, was the official trainer. She had 14 horses in all and the yard was a sight to see. It seemed to have been plopped on the plains and was part of an entire complex of yards, paddocks, bungalows and the odd house which had once been in the middle of nowhere. There was no necessity for planning permission of any shape, form, or description, I assure you.

An assortment of long, thin trees, as close to poles as one could get, had been lashed together with rope sealed with some type of tree gum, to form a basic structure. The structure, its roof thatched with palm leaves, had been arranged to form an open-sided rectangle, divided equally by more tree poles into 14 sections, with a further tree pole serving each section as a door. And there you had it – a stable block.

There was no flooring since the soil was sandy, so when the horses had eaten off the grass, they were each left with a natural sand bed. Two tree poles on either side acted as a partition for each stable, allowing the horses free access to one another; so much so that they could virtually stick their whole bodies through the gap. This they would do, quite amicably, to groom and scratch each other. Our Jockey Club would have had a complete fit had it been required to give the yard the all-clear.

In the central area of the yard was a long, stone water trough, piped into a natural spring. It was from here that the horses drank. They were brought out in threes and fours, depending on how many the African boys were prepared to hold at any one time, to drink their fill before returning to their respective stables.

I had been given their best two-year-old colt to ride. He was their pride and joy, and it was felt that he was going to be their best horse, even though he had not yet raced. He was a good-looking colt, about 16.1hh, and long in the limb. He appeared very athletic and also full of mischief. As I looked at him, he eyed me in return, as though I was something unusual. It struck me straightaway that he was very mindful, and also very intelligent. Just as I stood assessing his physique, confirmation, and type, so he assessed mine.

'He does tend to give the boys some trouble,' said Patricia. 'It will be wonderful to have someone like you who knows what they are doing to ride him. Then you can tell me what you think of his ability and his mind.'

Patricia did not ride herself, but there was no shortage of willing hands to offer their services. There was no method of being taught for the boys so they taught themselves, by trial and error. Those who had, or developed, natural balance, ended up riding and those who didn't ended up brushing, washing and watering the horses. Feeding, for some reason, everyone wanted to do, and there was a good deal of Swahili squabbling over buckets and hay. Perfectly prepared to muck in and get my given ride ready, I was met with stunned looks.

'No, no, no,' said Joseph as he snatched the bridle from my hand. He then tugged me by the sleeve over to the water trough and urged me to 'Sit! Sit!', which I did. He then proceeded to light one of my cigarettes which he duly handed to me.

Now I was bewildered. I got the message, but felt completely out of place, sitting there like Lady Bountiful on the edge of the stone trough under the blue African sky, watching my horse being groomed and tacked up by some five different boys. There seemed to be little order to exactly who did what; each just appeared to try and beat the others to the next part of the exercise.

Whilst this was going on, my horse, who did not have a name, kept his eye on me. It was a strange look, full of depth and private meaning, but I could not ascertain the meaning behind the gaze. I put it down to the fact that I must have appeared extremely bewildered and like a fish out of water, so, really, he was entitled to eye me in such a manner.

Patricia had finished issuing instructions over on the other side of the complex and now came over to chat. She seemed unperturbed by the fact that I was quite firmly parked like Lady Muck. There was obviously nothing strange about it, I deduced, as she parked herself next to me.

We chatted about England and racing, Robert and myself, her and her husband, and her horses; in between which she would break off to bark instructions in Swahili which would end squabbles or send a boy running to fetch and carry.

Finally, the horses were ready and all seemed to be in order. Patricia rose to her feet and I followed her example. She called for her car to be brought round and I picked up my skull cap. The two-year-old with no name was led towards the water trough by Gabriel. Picking up my cigarettes, I tucked them into my pocket, then twisting my hair up on top of my head, I put on my skull cap. Horse-with-no-name and car arrived at the trough simultaneously. I took steps towards the horse but, strangely enough, found my way barred. Two small boys of about ten years old had appeared as if by magic. One of them gave Gabriel a leg-up onto the horse, and the other opened the car door for me.

Sitting in a car, being chauffeured to the gallops, is not my style. I felt a complete wally with my skull cap on, no horse in sight. I couldn't decide whether to remove it and admit my mistake, or leave it on and pretend that this was how I normally travelled, being completely *au fait* with colonial protocol. I left it on. Patricia seemed not to notice at all and the conversation continued without even a blink of an eye.

Arriving at the gallops, I waited momentarily for someone else to make the first move. Should I get out, or stay in the car? I didn't have a clue, but, following Patricia's example, I got out.

The gallops covered a large area about a mile from Patricia's stables and approximately a quarter of a mile from the edge of the lake. The lake, I hasten to add, was vast – about 20 miles long and 18 or so wide. An oval circuit had been rotovated in the sandy soil to create a running track, about one and a half miles long in total. This, like the complex, just appeared in the middle of nowhere.

At the bottom of the gallops stood a middle-aged gentleman. Seeing Patricia get out of her chauffeur-driven car, he hollered in delight. 'I say, how the devil are you, old gal?'

'Morning, Charles,' replied Patricia.

'Good heavens! What's this rather smart young filly you've got with you?' He made a gesture towards me with the walking-stick that he held. He sort of pointed it first, then waggled it a lot, beaming all over his face at the same time. It turned out that he was not joking – this was him. What you saw was what you got.

His name was Charles Pilkington-Smythe and he had lived all his life in Kenya. He owned the entire complex where Patricia kept her horses, and it was one of his yards that she rented. He was terribly nice and friendly, and quite fun – once I'd got the hang of which era he was living in. He too had racehorses, and they were due to arrive at the gallops at the same time as Patricia's, which they dutifully did. I felt that their prompt arrival was a good thing since I should not have liked to witness the wrong side of Charles's tongue, or his use of language.

Watching the impressive-looking string of horses arrive through the acacia and thorntrees was a sight indeed. I almost felt that I was watching a cinema screen. The early morning African sun has a different quality altogether from ours. It brought from the warming ground a sweetish smell that lingered in the air. The horses were unshod, which lent a softness to each footfall on their approach, just audible above the excited chatter of their enthusiastic jockeys. I quite forgot that I was standing there with my skull cap on beside an ageing colonial and a cheery memsahib. I longed to be on horseback and to ride along with the lads, and ask all about this extraordinary land of theirs which seemed so timeless.

I did finally get to sit on horse-with-no-name. He was ridden right up to the very spot where I was standing. Gabriel dismounted and, at last, my skull cap had purpose. Once seated on the most horrendous saddle I had ever had the displeasure to sit on in my life, I was grateful for the fact that I would be on the gallops and would spend most of the time standing in my stirrup leathers. Having accomplished this mission, I awaited my instructions from Patricia.

'Now this is where he can be a little awkward, so what we've been doing is making him work on his own. It's good for him to get away from the other horses. So I'd like you to take him round the gallop once – not too fast – I think a half-speed will do and then let him lengthen coming back down the home straight. Okay?'

'Yep, that's fine by me,' I replied, gathering my reins and nudging horse-with-no-name forwards with my legs towards the gallop.

Horse-with-no-name suddenly became extremely flexible and bendy. He moved his hind limb forward, as if to march off smartly, but at the same time he brought his shoulder on the same side back, and sort of 'banana'd' in the middle – moving my body weight over to the left, and very nearly out of the side door.

'Mmm, that's a cute move,' I said to him under my breath, as I rebalanced myself and pushed him forwards again.

He moved off, again in the same fashion, only this time I was more aware. So, too, was he. I discovered, at this point, that he was most definitely ambidextrous. He completed the self-same manoeuvre, but to the opposite side. This time I found myself peering at his right kneecap, rather than his left. There was nothing dramatic in his dexterity; dramatic, I often find it easier to sit on. With him, it was the subtlety that made him so difficult. The bendy banana-ing, combined with the tightening of muscles here and there, made one feel like a tiddlywink – unattached and liable to fly through the air at any moment.

I became aware that all eyes were upon me. There was no sound now other than the trilling of the birds, as they dipped and darted from thorntree to ground and back, and the distant calls from the pelicans on the lake. I had no feeling other than that of 20 pairs of eyes all boring into me while I sat on the two-year-old with no name, whose vocation in life was quite obviously break-dancing and jive.

Gabriel rushed to my aid. He arrived at horse-with-no-name's head with the speed and agility of a gazelle, and began tugging at the reins. I believe that it was his intent to literally drag us onto the gallop.

I politely but firmly said, 'No. No, thank you.' I took up the reins again for it was clear that the horse had no real intention of unseating me. If he had, he could have managed it so very easily, but he had stopped short of depositing me both times. I was not his problem.

Puzzled as to exactly what his problem was, I nudged him forwards again, and he responded. He shuffled and banana'd his way, not, unfortunately, towards the gallop, but into an acacia tree. Wrestling with the branches which prodded me every which way, I said to him quietly, 'What on earth are you doing?'

I wasn't angry with him, just really puzzled. I knew he wasn't trying to get rid of me, and I also knew that it wasn't a joke – he was genuinely trying to deal with something. But what?

Then I became hugely aware of 20 pairs of eyes on me again. This time I could really feel them, all burrowing into me.

I could have slapped myself for being so slow. This was what he couldn't handle – being stared at, being the sole focus of everyone's attention. He was giving me the exact same sensation, the same perception as he had. I knew exactly how it felt to be stared at by these piercing eyes. Now I understood why he was trying to disguise himself as an acacia tree. Now it all made perfect sense. I'd missed the message first time round, but the second time, it had clicked.

'Got it,' I said to him patting his neck. I glanced back over my shoulder briefly, and there were, indeed, 20 pairs of eyes on us. Everyone was standing rock-still, silent, and calm. But they were all staring – wide-eyed and totally fixated. I remembered my mother telling me when I was a child how rude it was to stare. Never had she spoken a truer word I thought now, sitting on horse-with-no-name, entwined with an acacia tree. It was a deeply unpleasant sensation. We are all sensitive to this type of focal intrusion; there can hardly be a person alive who has not noticed at least once when they were being stared at. But if you felt that unpleasant feeling and multiplied it twentyfold, then you too would wish to be a tree.

It half-crossed my mind to ask everyone if they would please divert their eyes, but I knew that this would be far too complex a request requiring a lengthy explanation, and would be no solution, anyway. The only alternative, therefore, was to help horse-with-no-name to focus upon something else.

And so I talked to him – about anything and everything. I told him who I was and that I came from far, far away. I described to him my local countryside and the rides that I took my horses on. I told him anything that came into my head. I spoke very softly to him, almost murmuring, describing everything in detail to him as if he were a personal friend.

He came out from the acacia tree and walked to the gallops. I did not stop talking to him. I kept my focus entirely within my imagination, remembering all the things I could about home; all the things that I'd done the week before I'd left. And he joined me there, in my imagination.

Listening to my voice and my descriptions, he flicked his ears back and forth as he walked along the first stretch of the gallop. I gathered my reins and nudged him into a canter, still talking softly and slowly, as though describing a holiday to someone from an armchair. He responded, moving smoothly from a walk into a flowing, lengthy canter stride.

We began our journey up the gallop. He felt magnificent, his long, sculptured limbs reaching with ease across the rotovated soil, and his back contracting and stretching underneath me with every flowing stride. He did truly belong to this beautiful country. At first, I felt him to be like a greyhound, but then he felt more like one would imagine a cheetah to be. Such grace, such ease within each stride and footfall. He *was* poetry in motion.

I was soaking up this divine sensation, still talking to him softly about me and my life, when the warning split through the sweet African air like a high-speed bullet. It was the booming voice of Charles Pilkington-Smythe.

'I say, m'dear – forgot to mention it. Keep a lookout for hippos! Tend to sit on the gallop in the early morning, doncha know – what!'

Speaking quietly to horse-with-no-name as he glided into the first sweeping curve, I said, 'I think he said hippos. In fact, I know he did. If we meet a hippo around that top bend, I hope you can jump!'

I could hardly believe my ears. It was not what one could normally expect to be warned against when riding a big rangy two-year-old colt at a half-speed. It was as much as ours at home could do to cope with a pheasant or a dog, let alone an enormous hippo or two, basking on the ground.

Approaching the turn into the furthest section of the gallop, which could only have been a few hundred feet from the lake since the sound of the pelicans was growing louder, I braced myself to see a wall of hippos blocking our path. They seldom wandered around singly and it was far more likely that we should meet a whole family. If this turned out to be the case, then I was going to be lost for strategy.

I remembered having once jumped two sheep that had wandered into my path while galloping a three-year-old. He'd had the wit to jump, even though he'd never been taught. But how big was a hippo? I imagined myself looking for a stride on the approach to an open ditch; but in place of the fence I put a mental hippo, deducing from this that, size-wise, it would not be impossible – provided that the hippo stayed still and I had a clear run at it.

Horse-with-no-name continued, completely unfazed by my

hippopotamus ramblings and my advice on how to jump one, should the need arise. He glided easily into, and out of, the turn which led us into Hippo City. I hardly dared to look, but when I did, I saw, not hippos, but giraffe – four of them grazing the trees that lined this stretch of the gallop.

They were magnificent; huge, and close, so close. I had seen giraffe before, as I am sure many people have, but in that moment my air of complacency left me forever.

'Oh yes, giraffe. I've seen lots at the safari park and the zoo. Huge, great tall things that eat way up in the sky. Yellow with big brown hexagons all over them, and those funny little heads with stretchy lips and big tongues. Oh yes, I've seen those before.'

Well, look – and look again. Next time look properly and closely, I urge you.

These were young and probably not fully grown. Tall and elegant, they were picking away at the succulent young leaves on the trees. Two of them lifted and turned their heads from their meal at my sudden arrival, and stood still and watchful, but not alarmed or afraid. The third reached out his neck towards us as if to get a better view. But the fourth – oh, the fourth.

He stepped from between the trees and joined us! He seemed to move from the knee first, reaching out with his great cloven hoof and placing himself alongside us on the gallop. His stride was so light, so extraordinarily quiet for such a huge creature, and his small head rocked to and fro with the balanced swaying of his enormous neck.

Horse-with-no-name pricked his ears and moved smoothly up a gear. And so, too, did the giraffe. His great long, exaggerated steps made little of the ground. He just swallowed it up, stride after stride, yet he appeared to be travelling in slow motion.

I was absolutely speechless. I cannot find the words to describe the awe which beset me. It was the most remarkable experience, yet filled me with a sense of stillness, as though I were in another dimension. My mind was empty – empty of everything I had ever witnessed, learned or done. My entire world became the vision of this slow-galloping giraffe and the sensation of this graceful, gliding colt. Nothing else existed, and for those few short moments in time, nothing else mattered.

Coming into the bottom turn of the gallop, I eased horse-with-no-name back to a steadier pace – steadier and steadier as we returned to the others. He responded with the same smooth ease with which he had moved up through the gears, and came back to a free-flowing trot.

His breathing was strong and regular, but not harsh or tested. The air rushed in and out of his nostrils with the sound and sensation of exhilaration and joy. His slender frame felt lithe and supple, warmed and more flexible than ever. Back to a walk now, he marched jauntily up to the others, full of spring and vitality.

I was still awestruck and speechless. I wanted to blurt out all that I had felt and experienced, but I couldn't find the words. I must have been gaping like a goldfish, in truth. If I didn't look as such to Patricia, Charles, and the lads, then it was a miracle. For that was exactly how I felt – like a gaping guppy.

'Superb! Absolutely superb!' boomed Charles Pilkington-Smythe. 'Now then. I've got this little grey chappie here who is racing at Nairobi a week on Friday. I'd just like you to pop on him and give him a bit of a work-out with these other two.'

This was not a request, it was a command. Charles then began barking short, sharp instructions in Swahili and waggling his walking-stick in a fervent manner. It all seemed to make sense to those who needed to respond, and within a matter of seconds there stood beside me a little grey gelding, held firmly by one of Charles' lads.

Gabriel appeared with lightning speed at the head of horse-with-no-name and fastened himself firmly to the reins. The look in his eyes conveyed puzzlement as to why it was taking me so long to dismount. I, however, was still trying to catch my mind and bring myself back to earth.

The giraffe had continued with us down the back straight, but as the gallop had begun to curl its way towards home, he had taken his own line towards a plantation of tall trees. I had been unable to keep sight of him as our directions had diverged and he had become shrouded by those great, swaying giants. Just before the bend, we had parted company, like a dream having reached an unsatisfactory end.

How could I possibly regale these people with this. They must have seen it quite clearly since, standing here now, I had a good view of the back straight of the gallop. I looked at Patricia's beaming face. 'Did you see that giraffe?' I breathed, my voice long since having left me. I did not mean it as a mere question, but rather that someone else should confirm my dream for me, to keep it as a reality.

'Oh, goodness, yes,' she replied with an offhand gesture, flicking her right hand as if to remove dust from her coat. 'They do that all the time.'

Oh, I could have wept. Complacency – such complacency – of which we are all guilty. I made myself a silent, personal vow, there and then; never would I look upon our wildlife again with such complacency. Whenever I next saw a deer or a fox, a stoat or a weasel, an owl or a kestrel, even – or especially – a sparrow or a blackbird, I would make the effort to see it as something totally unique and special, to look upon it with as much awe and delight as I had looked upon that giraffe.

I did ride Charles's little grey, and whilst he went beautifully, he was unable to summon the grace and agility of horse-with-no-name. Thanks to the giraffe, I did not see him as anything lesser than horse-with-no-name, which I might easily have done. He was not as fast or as sensitive, he was not as athletic or as flexible, but I did not look to these things. I let my feelings have full rein, as if my mind were an open door. That way I would hopefully not miss the unique and special qualities that he possessed.

And they did come. They came flooding through as I sailed, once more, around the gallop. There was such an honesty about him – a workmanlike, earnest honesty to be felt with every stride. He focused all of his will and his ability into his work, without needing to be asked. His hold on the bit was respectful, almost polite. He did not pull in front of the others, or show reluctance to keep up; he went where he was asked, and at the speed he was asked. His little body worked hard and with determination and as a consequence, he went very well.

Charles Pilkington-Smythe was delighted. He all but insisted that I fly back to ride the horse in the race at Nairobi. When I declined and tried to explain that I had work to do at home with my own horses, he merely waggled his walking-stick. 'Pish and tish! I'm sure your chappies can manage without you for a weekend or so.'

When I explained that there were no 'chappies', just myself and another girl, his look changed to one of total disbelief. He was genuinely dumbfounded to hear that I mucked out, fed, groomed, rode, and drove the lorry myself. Poor Charles, I felt sorry for him. He not only looked bewildered, but completely defeated. He tottered off, scratching his sun-freckled head and muttering things that I could not hear.

All the horses having been worked and cooled off meant that it was time to go back to the yard – to which end the cars were duly summoned. No riding home here. The horses had their girths loosened and were led and we were driven. This time, I took my skull cap off.

As we bounced along the dirt track in the direction of home, I was still pondering the whole experience. It was certainly a unique one, and one that I shall never forget.

Patricia broke my train of thought, asking my opinion of her two-year-old with no name. I explained to her his attributes, wondering how she might be made to understand the fact that he did not like being stared at, that this would most likely be his undoing in a competitive environment. His stride and natural athletic ability made galloping very easy, but his sensitivity and awareness would almost certainly hinder him; unless, of course, she could find a jockey prepared to completely forget all prior education and just chat to him, about anything and everything, as he came up the home straight.

It was definitely here that he would have the most difficulty, for if the sensation of 20 pairs of eyes was so unnerving, I shuddered to think what effect 2,000 or so would have – particularly if those stares were magnified by binoculars! I decided that here in the car was not the place to try and explain such matters to Patricia, and since breakfast was next on the agenda, it might well prove to be a better alternative.

As we rounded a bend in the track, a sight came into view that made me catch my breath momentarily. Then I began to roar with laughter. For there, right in front of us, was horse-with-no-name – loose, stirrups and reins flapping – cavorting with a giraffe!

It may well have been the same giraffe, I couldn't be sure. But the pair were bouncing around swinging their heads up and down at one another; horse-with-no-name squeaking and executing bronco-style bucks followed by the odd rear; the giraffe skipping and bucking in slow motion, flicking up his heels and shaking his head so that great ripples of delight swung down the whole, great length of his powerful neck.

Following in hot pursuit was Gabriel, arms aloft and frantically waving; a string of garbled words beseechingly issued from his lips. Neither of them took a blind bit of notice of him. In their world he obviously did not exist. In fact, he might just as well have been a wild turkey strutting its stuff.

I could hold this vision no longer as tears of laughter streamed down my cheeks and blurred my sight. My sides began to ache and my mirth became soundless as I curled up on the front seat of the car. The driver came to a halt and Patricia leapt from the back to join Gabriel in the recapturing of horse-with-no-name. I couldn't sustain an upright position long enough to see who caught him, or how he was caught. I was far too consumed with rocking back and forth and catching the odd gulp of air lest my lungs collapse.

When the horse had been retrieved and suitably chastised, and the giraffe shooed away, my laughter died abruptly – as does a flame in a gas lantern when the supply is closed off. It just died away leaving me feeling as though I had never been laughing at all. What was perhaps more alarming for me was that, looking at the scenario now, it no longer seemed in the slightest bit funny!

I coughed and spluttered a bit as Patricia climbed back into the car, regaining my composure with the aid of a cigarette.

'Hopeless!' she exclaimed. 'Absolutely hopeless! I'll bet you don't have these problems with staff back in England.'

'Er, no,' I replied, 'strangely enough, we don't.'

We set forth again, a result of Patricia's command to the driver. As we passed horse-with-no-name being led along by Gabriel, I glanced at him and he at me. And then I knew – beyond a shadow of a doubt.

And if someone ever asks me, 'Do horses laugh?' I will answer, honestly and sincerely, 'Yes. Yes, they do. They really do.'

12

A Bed, a Bath and a Massage

Travel is a wonderful thing, and so easy in this day and age. Coming home on the plane made me appreciate the whole extraordinariness of it. Just think, I could get in my car and within nine hours be up in the tip of Scotland, or board a plane, and in the same amount of time, be in Africa or some other equally exotic place thousands of miles away.

I have always enjoyed travelling and with Robert and Jackie's organisational expertise, saw great expanses of the English countryside that I might never have seen, had it not been for the endless cries for help coming daily down the phone. Jackie had kept in touch since our propitious meeting on Emma's riding course and since returning to England from her stint in Switzerland, had come to help with our ever-growing workload.

All the needy animals dotted far and wide gave me the opportunity to stay in some fantastic places – and some horrendous ones. As I drove from one location to another on my visits, Robert would ring me with details of my overnight accommodation. His usual line of thought was to book me in somewhere close to the location of my final appointment. Being a real morning person, Robert himself would choose to drive a short distance, stay overnight, and spring early from bed the following morning to complete the journey to the first client of the new day. I, on the other hand, am more of a night person. I much prefer to complete a lengthy drive to my guest-house, long into the night if necessary, and crawl from my bed at a civilised hour, preferably on the doorstep of my first appointment.

We often argued as to which was the better and healthier option, each of us holding fast to our own preference. So sometimes I had things my way and sometimes Robert would just not budge, and would arrange accommodation as close as possible to the yard of my final client, insisting that I take more time to rest in the evening. Then in the morning, he would ring me, again and again, just to make sure

127

that I was awake and up, knowing full well that I would still not have got an early night.

On one particular evening I had got my way and I was glad, for I found myself driving through the Peak District national park. It was one of those cold nights in early spring; cold but very, very still, as though the air had ceased to move. There was not a house light or another car in sight, only the dramatic rise and fall of the landscape, bedecked with thick heather and all lit up by the most glorious full moon. The moon appeared to hover just above one of the highest peaks, showering beams of silver over the heather carpet and filling the sky with its soft, translucent light.

It was a stunning sight and I felt compelled to pull over and get out of the car. I stood there, completely alone in the silvery heather, under the watchful gaze of the moon, listening to the stillness. I lifted my face to the sky, tilting my head back as far as it would go, and closed my eyes.

I have no idea how long I stood there, but with my eyes shut I could feel the moon. I could feel its warmth flooding through me, through my whole body and down to my feet, embraced by the springy heather carpet. I felt one of those profound sensations that sets one's body tingling and glowing all over, causing the small soft hairs on the back of one's neck to rise, and sending shivers down one's spine.

This is why I am a night person. This was why I wanted to stay there for ever.

It occurred to me that this must be how the rabbits felt every night while we were in the pub or watching television. This was the light that guided the fox across the heather in search of carrion; this was the warmth and watchfulness under which the sheep and cows could doze and feel safe; this was the energy which would seep like liquid into the flowers of the heather, through their stalks, and deep into their roots, replenishing, feeding, and empowering them.

I suddenly felt very guilty for being late to check-in at my guest-house, and knew that I would not be able to excuse myself satisfactorily. 'Sorry I'm late – I was communing with Mother Nature,' would probably convince the proprietor of my impending madness. However, it could not be helped. I'm afraid that whenever I am faced with an opportunity such as this, I have to embrace it with open arms, lest it be gone forever.

Reluctantly, I continued my moonlit drive along the narrow winding roads at about 25 miles per hour, with the car windows wide open. Eventually, I found myself spiralling down towards the town of

Buxton, nestling between the folds of the hills. During my descent I could see all the lights of the town, orange mingling with white, creating an illumination that rose halfway up the surrounding peaks. This was nectar for the eyes but, for me, could not compete with the moon.

I found my allocated guest-house and although I was much too late for the set evening meal, the proprietor, Marjorie, very kindly insisted that I should have something to eat. She prepared me the most wonderful salad, apologising for the fact that it was only a cold meal. I didn't mind at all; it was delicious, and a surprise since I had forgone any expectation of food the moment I'd stepped out of the car into the moonlight. Marjorie and her husband were not local and had purchased their property some five years earlier. They seemingly understood my compulsion to commune with the moon – either that or they were both extremely polite!

I went to sleep that night with the curtains open, hoping to catch more of that beautiful moon. Unfortunately, my window faced the wrong direction, and I had to console myself with the tail ripples of light just visible on the furthest peaks. I slept well and awoke late, narrowly missing breakfast.

Allowing the car engine to warm up, I scanned my map and directions at the same time as rolling a cigarette. I was not sure that I would make my appointment on time, but I guessed that I would be close enough. Cigarette lit and car ready, I set off.

I was due at a riding school situated in the Peak hills somewhere near to Congleton. It was a family-run business and a very busy one. Husband and wife team, Ruth and Richard, had bought an old farm and, between them, had successfully established their riding school. Richard was a very skilled rider and had evented in his youth, while Ruth was an instructor, qualified by the British Horse Society. All in all, they had four children, three daughters and a son aged from four to 14, and about 30 horses – not to mention all their dogs.

Their place had a busy and manic atmosphere, but a very friendly and welcoming one. As soon as I arrived, I knew that I liked being there. Ruth had asked me to come, not for all of their horses but for two in particular. She had also organised a clinic at her yard for other horse and dog owners in the area who needed my help. As a result of her organisation, I was scheduled to stay for two days, both of which were crammed with appointments.

Ruth had seen to it that each client had been given an appointed consultation time within the two-day schedule – much to Robert's relief and delight. This was no mean feat. Robert was used to organising my bookings but it involved all manner of complications: plotting routes to accommodate as many people as possible in an area, ensuring that directions were accurate, and juggling appointment times to fit in with the commitments and prior engagements of clients.

Ruth, on the other hand, had been strong and emphatic; it was two-thirty or not at all. After all, one doesn't tell the vet or the farrier that one has to pick up one's dry-cleaning or wait in for the washing-machine repair man.

And so it was. People arrived like clockwork at their appointed time, either transporting their animals to the yard to see me, or taking me to see their animals. Ruth organised like a demon, instructing clients – phone in one hand, schedule in the other – that I would be ready in ten minutes, as soon as I had finished my cup of tea and cigarette; or, if a consultation was beginning to overrun, that I was needed by my next client. She also cooked me lunch and supper, plied me with endless cups of tea, and organised the financial side of things. She was marvellous.

At the end of the first day, we sat in front of a roaring fire with a glass of wine and talked horses and dogs. Richard, Ruth's husband, was a huge strapping chap who knew his stuff. He took the rides and also gave lessons. He knew his horses inside out and spoke about them to me with passion and pride. But I also detected a sense of longing, and as he continued speaking it became apparent that he had never realised his heartfelt ambition. He was very talented and had evented successfully in the past, but due to commitments and life in general, his dream to compete again had had to take a back seat until other matters had been put in order, and he had the time and the resources to resume his passion.

He now had the horses and the facilities but not the time and he said that he felt that he was losing the inclination. I didn't feel that this was entirely true. As he had spoken, his voice had changed – just a fraction of an octave – and his handsome features had momentarily lost their glow, the light fading a little behind his eyes – to me, an indication of the loss and disappointment buried somewhere deep within his soul.

But his face brightened again, and the light returned to his eyes as he started to tell me about one horse in particular. It was obvious that he adored her, and he told me how he would find himself emblazoned with anger during lessons if his pupils took too strong a hold on her reins, or allowed their body weight to interfere with her movement.

I could identify entirely with his point of view, but could also sympathise with his pupils. It can be terrifying to be in the presence of someone who can execute difficult ridden movements with ease, knowing that, never in a million years, could one come close, oneself, by comparison. Having seen Richard's photographs on the wall – testimony to his skill – I could picture his tall imposing frame pacing the surface of the outdoor arena, his face furrowed with frustration, as he tried to impart words of wisdom and instruction to some lesser mortal, whose length of spine probably far exceeded their length of leg and who, despite all their compassion and sensitivity, would be the last person to ever achieve perfect balance.

Such matters could not have made things any easier for Richard, and it must have reinforced the weight of his disappointment to see his special and talented mare reduced to receiving these manual insults while he stood on the ground rather than sitting astride her. It could make no difference how many times he demonstrated the movement or the jump, the pupil on his horse would never be able to replicate exactly what the master envisaged.

Listening to Richard, it struck me how surreptitiously one's dream can be reduced to rubble. Richard was not a miserable or a morbid man; he was energetic, committed, and charming. And so, rather than allow himself to become embittered, he had changed his priorities, leaving his broken dream on the shelf to gather dust.

Richard now retired to bed and Ruth confided to me that I was honoured; normally he would have been asleep some time ago, for he was an early morning man. Although time was getting on, Ruth and I continued to chat. She began talking about her involvement in the re-homing of rescue dogs. She explained how she took stray and homeless dogs from the overcrowded rescue shelters, and introduced them to family life among her own dogs and children. When she felt that she knew and understood them sufficiently well, she would throw her heart and soul into finding the very best of homes for them.

She had an album of photographs, all of the most beautiful dogs – some splendid and handsome, some cute and cuddly – and all of which she had, through her endeavours, managed to re-home with people who loved and cherished them. While this gave her a tremendous sense of satisfaction there was always a never-ending stream of them, huge almost unaccountable numbers that just kept coming, and for every one that Ruth failed to rehabilitate successfully, a tiny piece of her self-worth burned out. For she worked very hard and was also very intuitive, trusting her feelings that a bond could be made between each dog and new owner.

At what point would the vast numbers of these stray animals decline into something much more manageable? It all seemed so endless, like a treadmill, and she was beginning to feel that all her efforts were no real solution at all, for no sooner had she re-homed one, than there appeared another five in need.

I could sympathise entirely for it must have been very debilitating for her at times. We discussed the benefits of spaying bitches and neutering dogs to prevent such wastage. Whilst this is very much the policy of any rescue group, it did appear at grass roots level, that the numbers were on the increase rather than the decline.

We finished the last drops of our wine and, looking with horror at the clock above the mantelpiece, decided to make tracks to bed. Ruth had warned me earlier that my room might not be quite what I was used to, but I did not let this faze me; it could not be any worse than some in which I had found myself ensconced.

Collecting my overnight bag from the car, I paused momentarily to look up at the sky. It was moonlit and starry, having the same mesmeric quality that I had encountered the night before. I closed and locked the car door, telling myself firmly not to get into communing mode again, for Ruth was waiting for me at the front door of the farmhouse.

Walking back to rejoin her, I could not help but think how lucky her horses were to be roaming the fields free on such a night as this. I knew that the area also bestowed some harsh weather upon them from time to time, but nights such as these last two must surely replenish and sustain their hearts.

As I followed Ruth up the stairs, she said, 'Now I did say that you would be sleeping in the bath tonight, and you'll see I'm not joking!'

She opened a little three-quarter-sized door and ducked under a low ceiling beam as she went through it. I followed, dying to see what was inside the room. As I entered I feasted my eyes, for it was indeed a bathroom, and quite a large one at that.

The room was high up in the farmhouse with a low ceiling that sloped down on either side from the highest point. In the centre was a yellow bathroom suite, fully operational and plumbed into the wall that divided this room from the next. In the right-hand corner, up against the wall and directly alongside a narrow rectangular window, Ruth had put, and made up, a bed.

'Now this is what I call en-suite,' I said, looking around. No need here to stagger the length of a corridor in the middle of the night, tentatively checking every door in search of the loo; no need to worry about forgetting my toothbrush, or fear a takeover by another guest should I run back to get it. This was wonderful; everything I could possibly need in one room.

I said as much to Ruth, and meant it. She looked relieved that I didn't mind, and hastily explained that the facilities were for my exclusive use since there was another bathroom downstairs which she and her family would be using.

We said our goodnights and I must say I had an excellent night's sleep in 'the bath'.

The following morning the family was already up and about by the time I descended the stairs to the kitchen. The older children getting ready to go to school. Rachel, the eldest girl, who was tall, fair and very pretty, was simultaneously finishing her homework and her breakfast. She was a lot like her mother, aside from her hair colouring, and whilst Richard was wide awake, having already been outside to catch and bring in the horses that were needed for work that day, Rachel and Ruth were not altogether there yet – much like myself.

Suddenly Rachel remembered something that she needed for school besides her finished homework. Startled into wakefulness and sensitive by nature, she became upset and began a frantic search, rummaging through school-bags and cupboards, and running up to her bedroom and back to the kitchen.

Her younger sister, on the other hand, had been awake and with it for some time. She had a cute impish face and a complete devil-may-care attitude. She had woken up full of questions for me about her pony that she had forgotten to ask the previous day. Showing me the scar covering the area where her spleen should have been, she reinforced the fact that she had forgiven him his sins against her.

The youngest daughter, Emily, who was only four years old, seemed quite happy to amuse herself, and was busy long-reining the terrier around the kitchen, looking for all the world as if she would be following in her father's footsteps, but with her mother's love of dogs. It was the wit and aptitude of this four-year-old that had us all in stitches that evening over supper.

Ruth explained that while I had been busy with my final client, she had seen her small daughter standing in the middle of the yard with the terrier. She had been lightly holding a short stick of uncooked spaghetti between the fore and middle fingers of her left hand. This she had placed purposefully between her lips, then, taking a long hard pull on her imaginary cigarette, followed by an equally long exhaled breath of deep satisfaction, she had declared, 'Yes. There is something wrong with this horse. It seems to be hurting here. And here.'

At this point she had placed her hands on her stomach before continuing. 'Let me see. I think I know what the problem is.' She'd paused for another draw on her spaghetti before a dramatic finish. 'Yes. It's going to have a baby!'

I thoroughly enjoyed my stay with Richard, Ruth and family and I was most grateful for their kind hospitality. I must say that I have been lucky, for they were not the only ones; many people have extended me the same honour.

One lady who had called me in to see her horse jumped up and down in a very excited manner on my arrival. 'Oh my goodness! You're here! I can't believe it! I really can't believe that you're actually here! Oh my goodness!' She clasped her hands to her cheeks, then pressed them together between her knees, then back to her cheeks again, bobbing up and down as she spoke.

I was stunned, and looked over my shoulder, half-expecting to see Mel Gibson or some other such star standing behind me. There was no one there, no Mel Gibson, Queen Mother or Lester Piggott. Then the penny dropped and my heart lurched in my chest. 'Heavens,' was my thought, 'I think she means me.' I had another quick glance over my shoulder just to double-check but, sure enough, there was no one else – only me.

I really did feel quite overwhelmed and very embarrassed. Not so much at this lady's reception but more as to how on earth I was going to live up to her delight at my very existence. I did not believe myself to be remotely deserving of it and so I became all of a dither emotionally and mentally.

This peculiar inner squirminess still hasn't left me, although I do struggle with it. It creeps up on me every time somebody says, 'I saw your photograph', or 'I watched your demo on the telly.' I cannot help it; I just go completely squirmy inside. I realise, however, having been the recipient of such attention, that I am guilty of having bestowed it myself, only in my case it was upon a famous horse.

I had first seen him on television and had found myself glued to the screen, mouth open, tears rolling down my cheeks, my whole being charged with, what felt like, an electrical current. When I finally got to meet him and, moreover, touch him, I could hardly contain myself. He was just breathtaking; mesmerising and awe inspiring. I couldn't take my eyes off him, nor stop the electrical activity that pulsed through my chest and stomach. I was meeting my own personal god in the flesh – Adonis reborn.

I stood in front of him, tingling all over, my eyes out on stalks, wondering if I dare breathe in the personal space of this glorious creature, let alone actually touch him. I lost all sense of time and space and, probably, a large degree of sanity. I had forgotten how I should approach him or where I should touch him. Would he be offended if I patted him? Perhaps he wouldn't like having his nose touched or stroked. Perhaps I should stand a little to the side, or perhaps that is something that he wouldn't like.

Instead of feeling relaxed and at peace in his presence, as is normal for me when faced with a horse, I found myself completely overwhelmed – choked, really. My mind swam back to the memory of his powerful frame surging over the ground behind the glass screen of my television set. It wasn't so much his extraordinary achievement that had so affected me on that day, it was more the way in which he had tackled the task ahead of him; with blinding courage, power, and total determination, each intake of breath propelling him off the ground, and each outbreath stretching the length of him further and further.

I felt my throat choking up again at the memory, and tears welled in my eyes – tears of humility – an expression of total admiration for this horse; this horse who stood before me now, sporting a woolly winter coat covered in sun-dried mud, and a bemused expression. He was a god – a god in the flesh – smelling of life and breathing warm sweet air into my face over his stable door.

My legs turned completely to jelly and the tingling in my bones flew to my stomach creating a swarm of butterflies – or moths rather – pounding, fluttering and bashing away at my innards. I still could not speak and my euphoria was becoming more and more heightened rather than diminishing. I told myself mentally to get a grip, but my body would not listen; it was super-charged.

I tried to create a noise in my throat, hoping that it would sound like, 'How can I help?' No such luck. The sound that met my ears was a faint strangled squeak. Swallowing and clearing my throat, I tried again. This time it was better, largely audible and vaguely comprehensible.

I was informed of the horse's difficulties. In spite of the fact that he was now retired, he was such a hero that his owner was prepared to do anything for his well-being. Whatever was possible, he could have.

I turned to the horse. Again my throat closed and I fell into a coughing fit, being brought back from the brink of suffocation by a series of hefty clouts on the back from a very concerned owner.

Regaining a fairly upright posture, I attempted once more to compose some semblance of intelligible sound with which to ask this most mighty of creatures how he would like me to help. The resulting communication must have come across as appallingly broken 'horse', but he got the message.

He was very puzzled and to a degree quite unnerved by my presence. He was very aware that I meant him no harm, but he didn't understand what on earth was going on with me. I wanted to explain but could not find the appropriate words. Had the words sprung to mind, they would undoubtedly have stuck very firmly in my throat, leaving me gagging and gibbering as before.

I resorted to formulating a sentence in my head. 'I'm very sorry to be standing here gibbering and shaking, but it's because you are the most magnificent creature I have ever had the honour to stand beside. I saw you on the television and what you did and achieved filled me with such feelings . . .' My message dried up there; it was impossible for me to explain. It was far better to let my feelings speak for themselves. Hopefully he would understand the honesty within them better than a formulated sentence anyway.

He did. He pricked his ears and stretched his fine nose towards me a fraction, suggesting that he was now at ease with me. Words returned to me in a faint whisper. 'What do you want me to do?'

The reply came as a sensation – strong and clear, precise and painful – a searing, stabbing pain which pulsed powerfully along my spine, stopping just short of my left kidney. It radiated through me three times, leaving me once again in a state of euphoric turmoil. 'He spoke to me! He actually spoke to me!' My mind reeled and the moths became more invigorated, while my legs renewed their trembling with a vengeance. He was more than magnificent; he was heaven and earth cloaked in sweet-smelling hair and mud.

I shook myself mentally. I really did need to get a grip on myself and restore some semblance of professionalism. I opened his stable door and took a step towards him, but thanks to my jelly-legs, I stumbled and tripped at the same time, reeling forwards at a pace I hadn't planned on. Flailing my arms in a windmill motion and bringing forward another jelly-leg to keep myself vertical, I ended up rushing into the stable right up to this, my four-legged idol.

He was shocked at my sudden antics and shied into the wall. Turning his head towards me, he snorted his surprise, sending another waft of his sweet hay-breath to intoxicate my jangled senses. I wished I could control myself, but it was just impossible. This horse was having a profound effect on me; my emotions had completely taken charge.

I managed to explain to his owner that there was a problem with the muscles of his back and he wanted me to massage them for him. I would therefore need something to stand on since he was such a tall horse.

This was arranged for me, and as luck would have it, allowed me four minutes or so in the fresh air to regain some sense of normality. I stood outside the barn and berated my senses for letting me down like this in front of my idol and his owner. I don't think they were listening, however, so I resorted to a cigarette, which certainly helped.

Straw bale in position, I found myself stroking and smoothing the horse's back as he directed me. Mentally trampling on my overawed emotions, I managed to chat to the owner at the same time as massaging this delicious warm muscle tissue, while another part of my mind kept flashing me replays of the glory I'd witnessed on my television.

I kept massaging and stroking, still in complete awe of the recipient of my ministrations. Then I received another instruction from him – one which made my blood run momentarily cold. He wanted me to hit his back. I had been rubbing and pressing the jammed painful area which he had liked very much, but now he wanted me to hit it – and quite hard too.

Oh my goodness. My senses were doing a back-flip somersault now, but I calmed them as best I could. Taking a deep breath, making a fist with my right hand and marking the spot with my left – I punched him! Yes. I punched my hero – right in the middle of his back!

The owner, standing quietly at his horse's head, looked up at me in alarm, and then quickly at his horse who was standing still and calm, ears flopping from the sides of his famous head. His owner glanced back at me, just in time to see me wince and take another strike.

'He won't like that, you know. He's quite likely to rear up. He did with the last chap who fiddled with his back – went right up, pulling me over – nearly came down himself. Skated right across the concrete, he did.'

Too late. I'd already got him with another direct hit. The owner sprang back and clenched his hand tight around the leadrope, this arm ramrod straight, the other clasped across his chest, scrunching a handful of v-neck jumper.

The horse didn't move. He stood with a blissful smile and twiddled his ears from side to side. It seemed that I had done a good job, but not quite good enough. He wanted more, but harder – much harder.

'Oh, my God,' I groaned inwardly, 'are you sure?'

For reply, I received another sensation in my own back – better but certainly not gone. Taking another deep breath and making a fist, I struck again, only harder. And again. *Smack!*

That one got it. There was a strange popping sound from underneath my left hand that I felt more than heard. A ripple ran through the horse's spine and up his neck. Shaking his head with a shudder, he simultaneously took an enormous breath, expanding his rib cage to massive proportions and causing his spine to reverberate; each vertebra twanging and snapping one after the other like a domino train. He finished with a great snort down his nostrils and a long slow satisfied sigh.

I stood still, poised on my straw bale. Owner stood still, poised on the ground, clutching his horse, mouth agape, amazed that the response had not been the more dramatic one he'd been expecting.

Now I really was speechless, so much so that my senses had shut up and were finally paying attention. The horse was happy – truly, really, relaxed and happy. His pain had gone.

Looking at him standing there, I could see that his back had changed shape; it was broader, softer, and flexible. Where previously there had been tight, bunched muscle, was now soft springy tissue. His neck was softer and definitely longer, his elegant, sculptured head appeared smaller and finer than ever, and his ears swivelled even more freely as though in freshly greased sockets.

But could I trust my eyes? I really didn't believe that I could, especially taking into account my actions. So I double-checked. 'Are you okay? Are you really all right? Has it really gone?' I semi-whispered, my voice coloured with my own disbelief.

His response was the final straw. A huge warm tingling wave of pleasure seeped tantalisingly up from my feet, like a swelling tide – something akin to melting ice-cream sliding over one's tongue on a blisteringly hot day. This divine sense of sweet pleasure rose higher and higher, up through my limbs and stomach, to curl itself along my spine, pausing to kiss each vertebra in turn as it travelled upwards. Where had been sharp pressing pain was now the sweet song of bliss – liquid bliss.

My emotions had reached an end. My eyes brimmed with tears again, my scalp prickled and tingled. And my stomach? Well, my stomach just folded – completely dissolved into a fluffy nothingness.

I still had my left hand on his back. Looking at it placed there, I knew that that was it. I had met him, touched him, felt him; I had spoken to him and he had spoken back to me. I was surrounded by his breath and his smell, and filled with his feelings of gratitude and thanks.

Yes. That was it. I would never wash again!

13

Mister Man

I drove home on cloud nine, flying along the road, way exceeding the speed limit. But I didn't care. I swooped round bends, flew up hills and glided down them, hanging onto the wonderful feelings I had been given by my horse-hero, lest they leave me for ever.

Home seemed to arrive all too soon, and I did my best to explain to Robert what had happened, trying to put my euphoria into intelligible words. He brought me back down to earth as gently as he could, explaining that he had taken a call from some people with a dog that had a cancerous growth on its neck.

An exploratory operation had revealed that the growth was in an advanced stage of development and, due to its location and size, further operations were deemed impossible. The dog's owners had explained that they were coming to terms with the awful news, but would dearly love to give their dog the opportunity to speak for himself, in terms of how he felt, or what he wanted. I clutched onto my euphoria, but, nevertheless, really did feel for the dog and its owners in their plight.

Their appointment was arranged to be my last of the day. The dog turned out to be a springer spaniel, delightfully friendly, with big smiley eyes, set wide apart in a chocolate-coloured face, which exuded warmth, in spite of his condition. His owners were lovely people who, despite their personal upset, had resolved to make the remainder of his life as special as was possible.

It always strikes me just how strange serious illness is. It seems to either create an extra-special bond between people and their animals, or a huge divide, leaving the people or animals concerned feeling completely bereft and unable to cope with the knowledge of it, far less the impending loss. Lucy and Bill had been devastated when their vet had diagnosed the problem and had explained the severity of it to them. Such emotion comes from the heart and can never be hidden or truly overridden by positive thinking – no matter how much one tries to be strong or rational. However, their vet had recommended to them another vet renowned for his homoeopathic expertise, who had been able to do something really special for them. He had managed to lift them out of their despondency, filling them with the courage to be strong for their dog. He had also treated the dog, doing his very best for him.

It is, of course, so much easier to be objective and strong on behalf of other people and their animals, but never so easy where one's own are concerned. To Lucy and Bill's eternal credit, they had managed to draw the necessary strength from somewhere. And so I had been next on their list.

I sat on their sofa, drinking the ever-welcome cup of tea, with Roddy the spaniel pressed closely up against my legs, searching me with adoring eyes. I asked him whether he was comfortable with his illness or whether it caused him any distress.

He replied that it was itchy; itchy in his throat and nose, and around his ears and eyes. So, I scratched it for him. I scratched the tumour and the scar, scratched his nose and ears, rubbed his sinuses and his eyes. He loved it. He wriggled and pressed himself harder against my hand, groaning with delight. I explained to Lucy and Bill how he felt, and that this scratching was just what he wanted.

Lucy looked up in surprise. 'One of our other dogs always licks his face for him if he looks a little uncomfortable – right there – across his nose and eyes.'

She knew, the other dog. Apparently she would sit with Roddy's head between her paws and lick him until he fell asleep or the itching was soothed.

It transpired, as my conversation with Roddy continued, that he, himself, did not really know what to say. I found myself sitting there, hugging and scratching the dog, looking at Lucy and Bill and saying, 'I don't know what to say. I don't know what to say.'

Luckily they were completely unfazed by this, although I don't think they realised that this was the voice of their dog. Usually when this happens to me, I can feel the emotion that lies behind the words, but, in Roddy's case, there was no great underlying emotion – just the simple and straightforward statement, 'I don't know what to say.'

It was really very hard for Roddy, and I understood his perspective entirely. He had been a gun-trial dog, and a very good one. His whole life had been marvellous since Bill had rescued him from a quite unsavoury home some five years earlier, and trained him for trialling.

His adoration for Bill and all the people who looked upon him with admiration and pride, had become his whole motivation for living. The better he had done, the more people had stopped to praise and admire. When they'd looked upon him, and spoken about him, it had been with genuine admiration and respect – whether for his temperament, gentleness, speed or obedience – did not matter. What mattered to this dog was their praise, their perception of him. This was what made him a good dog.

But since the manifestation of his illness, things had changed. Those that looked upon him now, no longer saw his brilliance and beamed with admiration. They saw only the terrible disease, the unsightly lump with its tainted smell. Now, when people looked upon him, it was with sorrow and sadness. Some could not look, and even turned away, unable to face him.

Of course, he did not know what to say. What could he say? The stroking and petting that had once been filled with warmth and pleasure, now felt only of the terrible weight of sadness and despair. His regular vet, he knew, had been filled with horror at her findings, and now looked at him with different eyes.

So I stroked and rubbed that tumour. I caressed and smoothed it – that horror – that *thing*, that had changed his life so dramatically. I touched it, and rubbed the smell of it over my hands, and drank my tea.

I explained to Bill and Lucy that this was what was needed; this touching, caressing and handling. If there was anything that could make a difference, then it would be this.

Such a simple thing – simple for me, for he was not my dog – not so simple for them, but possible. Lucy declared in a bright positive voice, 'I can do that. I really can do that for him. I can put the radio on and sing to him, and stroke and scratch him for hours on end. I used to love doing it – I can do it again.' She spoke with renewed courage and a sense of purpose.

Roddy got up and trotted round the room, wagging his tail vigorously. Then he shivered; a shimmy that started at his nose and, gathering momentum, travelled down the full length of his body. His eyes took on a new light; a slightly warmer colour; an added depth to the conker brown.

And Bill, he wanted to do something for Roddy too. So I asked the dog to describe his favourite walks. I passed the information to Bill, who recognised them. He declared his role to be that of taking Roddy to his favourite places; to let him run and play with the other dogs. He asked me, moreover, whether Roddy would like to continue his trialling exercises with the dummy pheasant. The reply was a resounding 'yes', and Roddy flopped onto the floor, baring his belly and throat for vigorous scratching, to which both Lucy and Bill responded.

I knew that it would be hard for both of them, but perhaps with practice it would become less so. It was easy enough for me to advise them, in my capacity as objective consultant, but when it is one's own animal in question, the love and friendship can go so deep that it can feel as if a part of oneself is dying.

I wished them all the luck in the world, and, as I left, I realised the importance for these two people of being able to do something for their dog. They were not vets or healers, but they had the capacity to give Roddy more than they might ever realise. They could give him their love. For it was this that he lived for – their pride, admiration, and love for him. And if they could give that same love to his illness and the tumour – then, who knows? Stranger things have happened.

It was a long drive home for me that night. It was late and very foggy, and so I treated the roads with the care and respect that they deserved. My mind resumed its ever-wandering role and I remembered, very clearly, something important that had happened to me as a child.

We had lived in Cyprus, and it was part of my father's role there, as an army doctor, to visit the leper colony once a month to conduct health checks and make sure that all was in order. Whenever he returned from one of these visits, he would be carrying great bags of oranges and lemons, boxes of artichokes, or cut flowers – all gifts of appreciation and thanks from the occupants of the colony.

On one particular weekend, my family was driving to the other end of the island, not too far from the colony itself, and my father stated his wish to call in, since one of the elderly occupants was not at all well.

We pulled off the strip of cracked tarmac which cut across the baked landscape and served the island as a road, but which, here in Britain, would have been considered no more than a smear of hardcore. Avoiding some lop-eared goats, which were foraging among the scorched, stalky tufts poking up through the parched earth, my father turned the car into a long gravelled driveway. The reduction in speed meant that the wind and sand that had swirled around the car's interior, keeping us pleasantly cool, was now replaced by the full searing heat of the day.

The driveway was surfaced with white chippings which glistened and twinkled in the strong sunshine. Bordering the drive, on either side, were hand-dug flower beds, brimming with flowers, mainly dahlias; great thick healthy blooms in bright yellow, deep red, cerise pink, and brilliant white, all nestling into one another, creating the most wonderful floral mosaic with their bright colours.

At the end of the drive was a barrier marking the entrance to the colony; a single metal pole, painted white, its free end resting in its forked hold, its cement-weighted fixed end, just yards from a tiny, corrugated-iron sentry box. Just before this was a big white sign sporting Greek and Turkish writing, rising up from a bed of flowering aloe vera plants.

The entire colony was bordered by a chain-link fence, about 12 feet high, topped by a single strand of barbed wire. My brother and I were in no way fazed by this. We were under the illusion that everyone lived in such fenced compounds. We certainly did, and my father worked in another, as did other people's fathers. If anything, it was a symbol of safety. A figure stepped from the sentry box and raised the barrier, seemingly recognising my father, and saluting him as we drove through.

We followed the gravelled drive around beautifully mown, small green lawns, all edged with white painted stones. From their centres, sprinklers spat jets of cool water, spraying across the manicured grass and in through the open car windows. This was a welcome relief since the plastic seats of our Peugeot heated up very quickly, and, when mingled with hot skin, caused our legs to stick, so that we would spend most of the time peeling our legs alternately from our damp body imprints.

We parked and got out of the car. Looking around, I could see flowers everywhere – dahlias and chrysanthemums, bursting from old crumpled oil drums and rusted and split tin cans. Round about were small groves of citrus trees, laden with fruit. Enormous oranges – plump and juicy – and bright shiny lemons dangled among dark green, glossy leaves. The manicured lawns and artichoke beds served to create lanes which led to rows of little huts, outside which were stacks of water melons, and trellises entwined with passion flower and jasmine vines.

The huts were built of baked brick bound with dried mud, several inches thick, and dented and chipped in places. The doors to each little hut were open, as were the shutters which served to cover the windows in place of glass. It was a beautiful little village and seemed to bloom with health and vitality, reflected in the fruit and the foliage.

An elderly gentleman came out of the hut nearest to us. I could not tell how old he was since I was only about seven, and when one is seven years old, everyone else seems old, even if they are only 16. He stopped, and stood just outside his front door. His face was filled with delight and he waved to my father, calling him over.

We went into the hut as a family, and he bade us all sit down on his simple chairs. His hut was cool inside and smelled sweet with the scent from the vines. He desperately wanted to make my parents a cup of coffee on his little stove, but this task gave him great difficulty. He had hardly any hands left; his fingers were gnarled and twisted, the skin covered in angry red blotches. It was impossible not to notice the discrepancy in finger length. Some were barely existent, while others were only two-thirds there, but flaking and obviously retreating. His face was the same – adorned with those livid red sores; shaved and furled across his cheekbones, around the edges of his lips, and across his nose.

His delight at having us there was so apparent. In spite of his obvious pain, he managed to make the coffee for my parents, and brought out a little tray of boiled sweets for my brother and myself. He offered me the little dish, but, as his hand came level with my face, I shrank back. I did not wish to, but something made me recoil slightly. As soon as I had, I knew, somehow, what I had done, and I looked up into his eyes.

The hurt – the real hurt – was so profound in his eyes, just for a split second. Then he shrugged and smiled, making what I took to be an excusing gesture for me, so that he didn't scare me any further. He set down the dish of sweets and indicated that we should take one if we wished. I did. I took one and put it in my mouth. But I could still see the hurt in his eyes.

He showed us his most prized possession. It was in a box on top of his wardrobe. He struggled to get it down, and so my father reached up for him and lifted down the shirt box. He placed it on the bed and opened it. Inside, tenderly wrapped in tissue paper, was a football shirt; emerald green with a white collar and a four-leafed clover embroidered on the left breast. On the back, in bold white embroidery, was the number nine.

This was his football shirt. He had been a professional footballer, and, as he held the shirt up against himself, one could still see the footballer. He was still there – behind the eyes – behind the disease. I couldn't see the hurt in his eyes now. I could only see the pride.

It was impossible for him to fold his shirt, so my mother did it for him, carefully wrapping it back up in its tissue paper and replacing the box lid.

We left that little house with a bag of oranges and a water melon. I left that colony with the memory of the hurt in those proud eyes.

Bless you, Mister Man – whoever you were. It is because of you that I was able to help that dog. What I couldn't do then, I can now. Thank you.

14

Precious Words

I had an idea once, one of those strange little ideas that just suddenly pop into one's head. What would happen if we were given limited words to use? What if, when we were born, we were allocated a finite number of times to use each word during our lifetime? How would we use them, I wondered. Would we use them with care and caution, treating them as something precious and special? Or would we gobble through them as we sometimes do a whole packet of biscuits, and have to spend the remainder of our lives using sign language?

Words are precious – very precious. Wonderful things can be achieved with words, but, so too can they do a great deal of harm. Maybe if words were rationed, we would store them up, and use them only on special occasions or to say only kind things, afraid to waste them or lose them. It is often only by losing something that we begin to appreciate its true value or recognise its importance.

If words were limited for us as a species, then we would have to learn to communicate by a different method. What would we choose? Mime? Sign language? Feel and touch? Who knows, we might even discover that we do not have the monopoly on communication after all.

It was an experience with one particular horse that prompted such notions to pop into my head.

Calico was a thoroughbred, and a favourite of mine when I was working in a particular racing yard. I do have a passion for the thoroughbred. I think it is because of their versatility; each one is so very different. Whilst among other breeds there are strong characteristic traits, the thoroughbred is like an open book. Individuality is their trademark, and Calico was certainly individual. He was about 16hh, dark bay, with a big white blaze – not all long and lean as some are, but square and butty. The role that had been chosen for him was hunter-chasing, to which he gave his heart and soul. Work was not his problem, but being caught was.

So long as he was out at grass, his temperament was delightful, but, if stabled, he became foul. His manner was not dangerous, as such, more unwelcoming and decidedly unfriendly. He would bite – not hard but just enough – and he would swish his tail and lift a leg to kick. He did not always connect, but when he did, it was with a sound tap – usually right on the shin bone – timely and well executed. Not a happy horse, it could be said.

So, because of this, we did our level best to meet his needs. After all, how could he race and do well if he was unhappy? So, unlike the majority of the yard's occupants, Calico went out in a field belonging to an ex-dairy farm, with copious quantities of lush green grass at his disposal. It worked a treat. His handsome face would light up like a beacon and he would charge off, bucking and squealing, then trot round with big springy steps, tail aloft. I loved seeing him like that. To me there is nothing more magnificent than a squeaky, bouncy horse. I would stand and watch him for as long as possible, soaking up his humour and delight. In such moments, all was well.

But come the evening when he had to be brought in – owing to concern for his welfare, and, of course, the fact that he was required for work in the morning – all was not so well. He did not want to come in. Not only did he not want to, but he bloody well wasn't going to!

We would traipse across the 40-acre field with goodies and treats, our buckets laden with delicacies – to no avail. We tried quad-bike, lasso and sheepdogs but to no avail. We sent an army of foot soldiers, linked by a selection of lead ropes, to surround him and head him into a corner – to no avail. This last, he sailed over time and time again. After all, if you could jump a four-foot hedge with a three-foot ditch in front of it at 30 miles an hour, without a care in the world then a three-foot-high rope, bravely waggled at your knee-caps, would hardly be a test of your jumping ability.

One evening, dishevelled, hot and sweaty, we trudged back to the house, collecting on route the discarded articles of clothing which lay strewn around the field. An air of melancholy gloom surrounded us.

'Doesn't look good, does it?' said Harry, one of the lads, 'ringing up Mr Noakes and telling him his horse won't be running at Devon and Exeter on Friday, on account of the fact that we can't catch him!'

This broke the spell of our sombre mood and we all burst out laughing, each of us imagining the owner's response. We cheered ourselves up by trying out variations of the hypothetical scenario on one another. By the time we reached the house, we'd ended up with, 'Hello Mr Noakes. Calico? Who? Never heard of him!'

Sitting in the kitchen, halfway through a cup of tea, I suddenly realised that I could catch him. So I said so: 'I'll catch him.'

The others looked up. They were not that surprised since I had a habit of saying strange things. Usually they just responded with blank looks.

'Well, good luck to you, then,' said Jimmy, topping up his mug of tea.

I downed my tea and set off back to the infamous 40 acres, armed only with a light headcollar and a lead rope. I had about one hour of daylight left.

I found Calico standing in the middle of the field. He was well aware of my approach and eyed me suspiciously. I took three more steps towards him, and that was enough. He began to walk purposefully away, his head turned slightly to the left so that he could keep a careful eye on me.

'Wait a minute.' These words flew out of my mouth quite by accident, not something that I'd chosen to say. Then I sat down in the long grass. Again, this was a subconcious, rather than a conscious, decision. Plopping down into wet grass on an autumnal evening is not strictly sound behaviour when trying to catch a 'won't be caught' horse. But, nevertheless, it worked. Calico stopped, and, turning sideways on, lowered his head and looked straight at me.

Seizing the opportune moment, I threw myself flat on my belly and started to squirm around on the grass with all the conviction that I could muster. I really went for it, squirming and rolling around with my eyes shut. I paused, after offering my very best, and peered up at him. He was still standing there, looking at me. So I began again, wriggling and writhing in the wet grass for all I was worth. I looked again. Yes, he was still there. And now he was eating the grass, tentatively, and with one eye very firmly fixed on me. So, the next step was in order.

I wriggled my way a few yards closer to him. He lifted his head, but he didn't move to make tracks. He just looked at me, head raised, as if to say, 'Carry on, I'm watching'. So I began edging towards him again. By now, my wriggling and squirming was full of artistic interpretation. I would probably have scored a 'ten' had anyone been watching, which, thankfully, they weren't.

The whole process took about 45 minutes. I wriggled and wriggled until I got right up to him. Then I lay on my back, looking up at him, waiting for his next move. His nose furled ever so slightly, his ears swivelled somewhat back, and he half-shut his eyes. Reluctance was written all over him. But he didn't move.

Well, that was okay. Now for my final effort. I writhed and slithered right beside him. I did not pay any attention to his response, for my heart and soul were fully focused on my command performance. When I felt that I had done enough, I reached out and closed my hand around his pastern, held it there for a moment, then climbed to my feet. Calico stayed put, standing right beside me, relaxed and appeased. I took the headcollar from my pocket and held it out in front of him. He dutifully, and without argument, put his nose inside it and let me fasten it up.

'Hoorah! What triumph!' I hear you cry. Well, let me explain. Yes, there was triumph – an enormous, overwhelming sense of triumph. But it was not mine. It was his. You might believe that it was my insane behaviour that had distracted him; or that he had believed me to be having some kind of seizure and felt sorry for me; even that I had bored him into a stupor. Well, no. The truth is – quite simply – that I had been grovelling!

Grovelling, grovelling, grovelling. I had pleaded with him and beseeched him for the best part of an hour – and not a word had left my lips. And I had done it with conviction too. I had had to be totally genuine or he would have seen right through me.

This grovelling was the only thing that could appease him. Instead of being dictated to, as was the norm for him, it was time for reversal of the species – horse over man. And quite right, too. After all, it was his skill and ability that we wanted so much, to boost our success rate, and to bring glory to owners and jockeys. So it was only fitting that we should be humble enough to respect him. Perhaps we should all get down on our knees, doff our caps, and, at least once, grovel to The Horse.

Back at the yard, we were greeted with amazement: 'I didn't think you'd do it,' 'I must be seeing things!' 'Bloody Hell, I'm gob-smacked!' I waited for the million dollar question, 'How?'

When it came, I took a deep breath and said, 'Well, I . . . er . . . um. What I did was . . . I kind of – sort of – hid in the grass . . . and ambushed him!'

Funnily enough, that seemed to go down very well. They could all cope with that, and from that moment on it was my job to catch Calico. Which I did. Paying homage, every time, on my belly in the grass. Sometimes for ten minutes, sometimes for 40. He deserved it.

Incidentally, at the Devon and Exeter races, he behaved impeccably, won the Best Turned Out prize, and finished a highly creditable third. When I collected him from the jockey, I held his ear, squeezed it

gently, and used just two words to him. Not 'Well done', or 'Good lad';
but 'Thank you'.

Appreciation, gratitude and respect are all wrapped up in the words
'please' and 'thank you'. Most of us use them with remarkable
frequency, but how often with any real meaning?

I had just landed at Jersey airport, having been requested to come by
some of the island's animal owners. The initial number of enquiries for
help had been too few to make a trip viable, but, thanks to Robert's
marketing efforts, I now had five client-packed days ahead of me.

It was July and the flight had been full. Negotiating my way through
the busy arrivals hall, I noticed a lady some way ahead of me,
struggling to keep a mountain of bags stabilised on her trolley. She was
simultaneously trying to attend to the needs of three tired and peevish
children. She appeared hot, flustered, and nervous. As she paused to
hand out pacifying sweets to her brood, she failed to notice her
handbag slipping to the floor from the over-laden trolley. She
continued on her way, unaware of her now abandoned bag.

Having only one medium-sized overnight bag to contend with, I
pushed my way through the crowds, rescued her bag, and set off in
hot pursuit. 'Excuse me!' I cried, running to catch her up. 'Excuse me!
Excuse me!' She appeared to be ignoring my cries. Glancing briefly
over her shoulder at me, she nervously whipped round and speeded
up in the opposite direction.

I renewed my efforts and managed to cut off her escape route. As I
drew level with her, her face registered worry and fear. I held out her
handbag, explaining what had happened. As my words sank in, I was
fascinated to see her features darken dramatically. She snatched the
bag from my hands. Her reluctant 'thank you' reflected no gratitude,
just huge relief that I had not done her any harm – as she had so
obviously feared – and anger and resentment that I had given her such
a fright.

'How interesting,' I thought, stepping out into the sunshine. I was
not offended but I so easily might have been.

It was the perfect time to be in Jersey. It is a beautiful island and I
was looking forward to rediscovering it, and finding out whether it
had changed at all since the time I had spent there as a jockey, gaining
experience to qualify for my UK licence.

Collecting my hire car, I realised that little, if anything, had changed.
My memory was rekindled by the street names and landmarks, and,
armed with my map, I found my way easily to my guest house. Since

it was the height of summer, accommodation had been difficult to book, and so one of my clients had arranged for me to stay at a particularly nice location.

My room was on the ground floor, with sliding glass doors leading onto a small paved patio, and from there onto the garden walks which were beautiful. Exotic shrubs and plants adorned the lawns and walkways. But the real treasure for me lay right outside my door in the form of an enormous and enchanting tree. It was truly a magnificent specimen. Its foliage grew tall, replenished by new leaves and budding shoots. I had no idea what type of tree it was, but that did not matter.

Throughout my stay, whenever I had the time, I would take a cup of tea and my inevitable tobacco, and go and sit underneath it. Sometimes I took my book with me, and although it was an excellent read, I found my attention increasingly drawn to the tree.

There was certainly something about that tree, and judging by the number of birds that adorned its foliage, I did not hold the minority opinion. It was most definitely live; a living, breathing entity, although, of course, it could never move. I imagined it to have stood there for as long as the island itself had been known. It will undoubtedly still be standing there long after my own existence draws to an end.

For it served such purpose. When I looked closely at its bark, there was life there in abundance. Spiders and insects busied themselves around its roots and up and down its trunk. A never-ending stream of birds, of all shapes and sizes, came to land in its branches, twittering loudly, only to fly off, returning a short while later. It was a hive of life, aside from that of its own. I loved the moments that I spent sitting beside that particular tree.

By the end of day two, word of my visit had spread round the island, and the phone began to ring constantly. One call came from a 14-year-old boy. He had an elderly pony, a problem dog, and about 20 or so birds, from finches to exotic parrots. He was very excited that I should come. I explained that I didn't know whether I could communicate with birds but that I was willing to try. I booked an evening appointment with him to fit in with his school hours and his part-time job in a pet shop.

As I replaced the receiver, I looked at the tree through the open door and thought, 'I'll bet you know more about birds than any of us ever will.' The phone rang again. This time I found myself conversing with a retired professor, a long-term resident of the island. He chatted for nearly an hour; about homoeopathy, and his experiences with animals, both here in Jersey and in India, where he seemed to spend a large percentage of his time whenever the Jersey climate became a little 'chillsome'.

He invited me to tea at the Imperial Hotel, an extremely plush and elegant hotel situated on the Esplanade with views of the park and Elizabeth Castle. I thought that this sounded quite delightful, so I agreed a time for the following afternoon, prior to visiting Russell, the boy with the birds.

I spent the last half-hour of fading daylight beside my tree, before retiring to bed to watch a film. The next morning I woke early, and surprisingly easily for me; perhaps due to the sea breeze that was blowing in through the still open door – or maybe due to the still blaring television. Never mind, for once, I would not be late for breakfast.

After breakfast I discovered that several messages had been left for me at the reception desk. The proprietor drew my attention to one from a Professor Farthing. 'Oh, yes,' I said. 'I spoke to him yesterday evening.'

The proprietor raised his eyebrows, just a fraction, and said in a very controlled manner, 'Ahh. So you have *spoken* to him, then?'

I replied that I had.

'But you haven't actually *met* him yet?' he retorted.

'No,' I replied, slightly puzzled.

'Ahh,' came back his reply. His face gave nothing away and had remained largely unexpressive throughout our conversation, aside from his ill-trained eyebrows. The telephone rang and he excused himself politely.

I hovered there for a moment. I was half-inclined to wait and ask for a little more detail, but decided against it. I have found that island communities can be a little over-zealous in their judgements of one another. Often such matters can be traced back six generations to when somebody's great-great-grandfather insulted, or stole from, somebody else's great-great-grandfather. I brushed any questions from my mind and went out to the car to begin my morning's appointments.

As I finished the consultation with my final client, prior to my tea-time engagement, I asked her the quickest route to the Imperial Hotel. 'Oh!' she sounded her approval, before giving me directions. 'It's lovely there – very smart. Don't tell me that someone has a horse ensconced in the hotel gardens for you to look at?'

I knew the island mentality well enough from my previous time spent here to realise that this was not an innocent question – it was a desire to know, dressed up as a quip. I also knew better than to try and fob her off with a return quip, since I would not be allowed to get away until I had satisfied her desire to know my business.

So I smiled and said, 'No, no. I'm meeting a Professor Farthing there for tea'.

'Ahh,' came her response. 'Um . . . Have you met him before?' This was delivered with feigned innocence.

'No,' I replied. To which she responded again, 'Ahh'.

The island need-to-know mentality was not, seemingly, balanced by a need to explain in return. And so it was with 'ahh' echoing in my mind that I set off for the Imperial Hotel tearoom. Driving along, I felt that it was a little late to do anything about the arrangement at this stage. 'If I don't like him, I can always leave,' I decided.

I found the only available parking space in the hotel carpark and considered myself lucky. I entered the hotel. It certainly was extremely plush. A thick, soft, royal-blue carpet sported the hotel's insignia in red and beige. The high vaulted ceiling was ornately gilded, and from it dangled weighty crystal chandeliers on thick chains. On either side of the wide hallway leading to the reception desk were arched alcoves displaying designer items with discreet labels such as Dior and Chanel. One held a single shoe and a coiled belt, both distinctively Gucci; another, three draped jewel-bright scarfs by Hermes.

I was beginning to feel just a little out of place, and more than unsuitably attired in my jeans and silk shirt. Usually I feel that these do the job admirably, but this time I was not so sure. On reaching the reception desk, I was greeted by Mrs Extremely-Glam, looking, for all the world, as though she were head of an exclusive Swiss finishing school. I suddenly felt as though my hair hadn't been washed for a week, and that my £4 tube of mascara was akin to using boot polish. She didn't bat an eyelid, and asked me politely how she might be of service.

I explained that I was meeting a Professor Farthing for tea, and asked whether she knew where I might find him. She was left no time to answer.

'Mrs Mackay!' A voice came from my right. Looking round, I could see no owner of this voice, only a splendid and enormous example of a cheese plant, potted in a beautifully ornate brass vessel. I just had time to mentally register surprise, before the leaves parted abruptly, and I was confronted by the voice's owner, literally clambering through the plant's foliage.

'Mrs Mackay. How nice to meet you.' I took the outstretched hand and shook it. 'Hello,' I replied, 'nice to meet you, too.'

He was a small, bespectacled gentleman, with a soft and gentle voice. He wore a pale, lemon-yellow shirt with three buttons missing, the cuffs undone and loosely folded halfway up his forearms, and one wing of its frayed and tufted collar sticking up at an angle. He had on plain black trousers that might, at one time, have belonged to a suit – although probably quite an old one, since the bottoms were slightly flared and swung freely just above his ankles. I could see his ankle bones quite clearly as they were completely devoid of socks of any sort, while his bare feet were wedged into a pair of black shoes that had once been very smart, but were now furled at the toes – the sole of the right one coming adrift from its well-worn, scuffed, leather upper.

Any concerns about my own attire had evaporated rapidly, the moment he'd appeared from out of the foliage. 'Shall we go through for tea?' he said, politely indicating the direction of the tearoom. I led the way and he filed in behind me.

As I rounded an ornate pillar, I couldn't help but cast a surreptitious glance back at the cheese plant. To my relief, I saw that there were two chairs placed beside it which had been hidden from my view when I'd been standing at the reception desk. Professor Farthing must have taken a short-cut through the foliage rather than walk around the plant, as one might be expected to do. I felt that he must just be a tad on the eccentric side of normal. 'But, then, what is normal?' I concluded in my mind.

We found a vacant table in the tearoom and sat down. But not before the good professor had surveyed every other alternative seating arrangement in the room, and had even contemplated reorganising some of the furniture to be closer to the window.

'No, no. This is fine, really. This is just perfect,' I said, clutching the back of a chair and pinning it to the floor, and planting my bag very firmly on the adjoining table. He acquiesced, and deigned to sit at the chosen table, although he did make it known that he considered it to be far too close to the tearoom door for his liking.

He ordered tea and tea-cakes, with relatively little to-do, but while we were waiting for them to be brought to us, his displeasure at being too close to the door got the better of him. He stood up suddenly, grabbed the table with both hands, and, with a swift tug, hoicked it away from the door and about a foot closer to the centre of the room. He followed up with another three or four tugs, until he seemed pleased with the table's new position.

My bag had been on the table, but, with the second tug, it had flopped onto the floor, spilling its contents onto the plush tearoom carpet. Professor Farthing appeared not to notice. But three-quarters of the other tearoom occupants did. Most tried to politely focus on their china tea cups and their linen napkins, but could not prevent their heads from turning towards Professor Farthing and myself.

The professor swiftly returned for the chairs which were still in their original position. He lifted first one chair, carrying it over to be reunited with the table, then the second, and then the third. Before I could register what was happening, I found myself sitting on a single, solitary chair by the door, looking at the space where the remainder of the ensemble had once been. Professor Farthing, having firmly ensconced himself in the new location, was now smiling across at me, apparently very happy with the results of his efforts.

At that very moment, our waitress returned with a large, polished silver tray, upon which sat our afternoon tea. Her step faltered briefly, and the merest hint of bemusement spread across her face as she tried to adjust to the sight of me sitting on my solitary chair by the door, with my belongings scattered liberally across the carpet. Her eyes scanned the room swiftly, and, spying our table, she regained her composure, deftly skipping over the contents of my bag on her way to set down the tray. 'Your tea, sir.'

I joined the professor and the tea at the table, carrying my chair and collecting my bag and its contents en route, determined not to meet any of the eyes that glanced curiously in my direction. Professor F. poured the tea. This seemed to go extremely well; the tea found its way into the cups, as did the milk, and the tea-cakes found themselves placed in the centre of the table – all without incident. The tearoom resumed its former state of serenity, and my cheeks their more natural colour.

We chatted about all manner of things. The professor was, indeed, a very interesting man. He held strong views on ecological matters, not to mention horticulture, medicine and first-aid, travel, and zoology. In conversation he had but one foible, and that was the emphasis that he placed on certain words.

As I described, his voice was soft and quiet – most of the time. But when he used particular words, a hidden volume control seemed to come into force, giving these words the capacity to travel the length and breadth of the tearoom, through most of the other occupants, and back to us. They reverberated and echoed, bouncing off the walls like a ricocheting bullet. No one within 200 yards was exempt from the effect of those words.

The first one caught me completely by surprise. We were talking about horses and oxen, and the very different roles that they both play in India, where they are used largely as pack and working animals. The professor had encountered some fairly horrendous flesh wounds from ill-fitting harness in his time, and, what with the heat and the fly population, the end results could be pretty spectacular. It was when he reached the word 'maggots', during a particularly vivid description, that his voice gained its extraordinary power.

Those who had been taking a sip of their Lapsang Souchong could be heard coughing and choking. Bone china teacups rattled violently in their saucers, while scones and fancies slid from silver platters to the soft carpet. All conversation ceased, save for that of Professor F. who had already resumed his normal, softly delivered tones. All eyes were upon us. But unsure as to who the exact culprit was, they glanced this way and that, sweeping the room before returning to, and remaining on, us. I guessed that it must be my wide-eyed, astonished expression and flame-red cheeks that had given the game away.

The professor continued with his tales, and, once again, the tearoom regained a sense of equilibrium. I began to think that maybe his outburst had been a one-off, like one of those hiccoughs that have a will of their own. I relaxed back into my chair, certain that all was now well with his tonsils. He began to tell of his time spent in the armed forces with troop horses; how they would ride for hours over some of the roughest terrain imaginable, and how, as a consequence, the horses were plagued throughout their gruelling careers with strained, lacerated ligaments and leg tendons.

He leaned forwards, earnest pride in his eyes, spectacles slipping down his nose. 'But, you know,' he confided, 'I managed to find the most marvellous cure – far better than any linament we had back in those days – URRRINE!! Marvellous . . . marvellous for tendons.'

I too had been leaning forwards in my chair, soaking up his every quiet word; his earnest pride drawing me closer, the better to hear every syllable. I should have learned my lesson from his first outburst.

I sprang backwards, almost shoved by the unadulterated emphasis placed on that resounding word. All around me, silver knifes clattered against fine china, tea was poured onto linen tablecloths, and strawberry conserve flew from ornate spoons into designer-clad laps. Coughing, spluttering, and back-slapping could be heard from every corner of that once serene, exclusive tearoom.

The professor was oblivious to it all. By the time the minute hand had completed its hour-long journey around the face of the gilded clock, he had let rip with other words for the benefit of everyone: 'RINGWORM!', 'SARCOIDS!', 'BOTULISM!' – and his finest – 'SCABIES!', to which he added extra impetus by drawing out the enunciation, although all were delivered with the resounding force of a cannon blast.

As we left the tearoom, I felt the urgent need to go and walk along the beach for a mile or two. I reckoned I'd just have time before my appointment with Russell.

Professor F. expressed his utmost delight at our meeting, and was emphatic that we should meet up again before I left the island.

'Somewhere for dinner,' were his parting words.

15

Sick as a Parrot

I drove along the narrow road, scanning the names of the houses, looking for the one that Russell had given me. Then I saw a young boy on a bicycle, frantically waving, a huge smile lighting up his face. This was Russell. He had been so excited that he had been unable to wait for me to find his house, and had come to meet me on his mountain bike.

He was addicted to his birds, absolutely fanatical about them. The back yard of his house was packed with aviaries full of different types: budgies, canaries, finches, parakeets, and cockatoos. The air was alive with their twittering and chirping, all different tones and notes, and all the equivilent of their words, their languages. They swooped and hopped from perch to wire, and back to perch again, and in and out of their nesting boxes. All busy and all very active. They had plenty of grain so they were not in a feeding frenzy, just busy.

I looked into one of the aviaries and wondered, just for a moment, what they were all saying; what their different sounds meant. What did it all represent, this mix of language, this hive of activity and sound? Some birds were still and largely quiet, some sang with beautiful pure clean notes, while others chattered and trilled, high-pitched and constant. They must be languages, I thought. But as far as I was concerned, they were ones that I didn't know. How on earth was I going to be able to communicate with all these different birds?

Then I remembered the big Muscovy duck at home; Mrs Miggins, we had christened her. One morning I had, quite by accident, mimicked her voice. She often made the usual duck-type noises, but particularly when the horses were being fed. She would waddle her way from the moat and, with fixed determination, cross the yard to the feed room, not in the least put off by our pack of dogs eyeing her in disbelief. On her trek, she would repeat the same series of sounds, over and over again. Becoming accustomed to these particular noises, we assumed that she wanted breakfast, or supper, and so we would feed her.

On this particular morning she had been fed and was happily paddling up and down the moat. I could hear her from inside the house while I made my phone calls. Somehow, I must have registered her exact tone and pitch. Unconscious of this fact, I gathered up my papers and left the house to go to the office. As I crossed the moat bridge, instead of saying my usual 'Morning, Mrs Miggins', I made a series of sounds that mimicked hers exactly, while thinking, as opposed to saying, 'Good morning, Mrs Miggins.'

To my amazement, I received in return, and quite spontaneously, a whole new series of sounds. Not many, but definitely delivered in response to mine and quite different from the 'feed me' voice. I stopped in my tracks and tried again. Mimicking her voice, I thought 'Can you understand me?' Again, I got a reply, different again and shorter than the first, but this time I understood it and knew it meant 'Yes'.

Something inside me lit up like a lantern. 'I just spoke Duck!' I exclaimed to Foxi who'd been looking at me with her head on one side.

Remembering this incident, I decided that it was definitely worth trying again. I would certainly give it my best shot.

I felt that it would be difficult to begin with such a busy and multi-occupied aviary, especially as a very excited Russell was chattering away as much as his birds. And extra-especially since he was accompanied by his highly suspicious mother – undoubtedly there to ensure that her son did not become the naïve victim of, what she suspected to be, a con. I asked whether we could begin with another aviary with fewer occupants. Russell was only too delighted to take me round the corner to where he had a pair of love birds. Mother came too, arms very firmly folded across her chest.

I stood at what I felt to be a polite distance from the pair of birds, and listened to their song. They had the most exquisite tones; the purity and gentle quality of their notes was beautiful. Recalling the sensation of inner peacefulness that I felt whenever I sat beneath the tree outside my room, I allowed myself to hear nothing but their sweet song. Russell was fabulous and stayed still and quiet. His mother shuffled her slippers, folded and refolded her arms, cleared her throat, and sighed a lot – but I had handled worse scepticism than hers.

When I felt that I had captured the sound clearly enough in my mind, I mimicked it. Not the range of their song, for I couldn't match that, but the theme note that seemed to hold their song together. At the same time, I asked in my head, 'Are you happy?' This was what Russell had most wanted to know.

They sat together on their wooden perch and nestled into each other. They blinked their little round eyes, cocked their coloured heads, over to the right, then down and over to the left a bit, and then back over to the right. From the little I knew about birds, this did seem to be a favourable response. Russell backed this up for me by saying, 'They're listening to you.' His mother shuffled and snorted her response.

So I tried again, replicating the same note and thinking the same thought. They listened again, and, when I had finished, they returned the sound. My first reaction was to think that they were mimicking me, but their tone had been slighty different. So I repeated the note, thinking this time, 'I did not understand that. Please tell me again.' This might seem an extremely long sentence to be condensed into a single note, but my mental emphasis was on the meaning of the sentence, rather than the words themselves. And it worked. They piped back the same note that they had used before. And this time, I understood the meaning. 'They are happy together,' I said, 'but they don't like the dog.'

I felt absolutely exhilarated. It was an astonishing and quite remarkable experience and, perhaps, purely personal. I felt a huge thrill of self-achievement. This was reinforced by young Russell who immediately said, 'Yes. That's right – they don't like him at all. Whenever he comes out they hide in their nesting box until he's gone. They get really upset when he barks and puff themselves right up. You can even see them squinting.'

His mother shushed him harshly, delivering a light cuff to his upper arm with the back of her hand. 'Don't tell her too much!' Then, in a semi-placatory tone, she turned to me and said, 'You don't need to know too much, do you?'

'No,' I said, not in the least offended for I was still high on exhilaration. I continued my sung conversation with the love birds, each of their replies validated and confirmed as correct by Russell – in spite of his mother's misgivings.

After a while, I felt that the time had come to bring the conversation to a close and said as much to Russell and his mother. Russell became a mite deflated. He had so obviously enjoyed conversing with the little birds through me. Then he brightened again, reminding me that he needed to ask that cockatoo something, and this zebra finch, and those parakeets – not to mention the dog and the African parrots that lived inside the house. I realised that this was going to be a long evening.

Mother's eyebrows rocketed skywards at her son's enthusiasm, and her slippers skidded to a halt. Not wanting to say too much to him in my presence but, nevertheless, determined to test me further, her suspicious mind flew into action. 'Ask them what they like eating best,' she demanded.

I winced at that one, and, I have to confess, nearly said 'Bird seed'. But I decided against it at the last moment. I asked the love birds, in the best way that I could, what they most liked to eat. My message got through, but they seemed to disregard the question. For what I received by way of reply was more suggestive of something that they needed, rather than something that they already had.

Now I was stuck. I knew that I had understood them correctly, but I could not work out what it was that they actually wanted. I tried once more. This time they became almost excited. Whatever this food was, it was obviously important to them. But I could not get it. I suspected it to be some kind of nut, but none of those that Russell suggested seemed to exactly fit the perception that I had been given by the birds. In the end, I had to admit defeat; more to the birds, really, for it was their loss.

But Mother bucked up no end at this. She unfolded her arms and the deep furrows on her forehead almost smoothed out completely. She had me. And I knew it. There was no way that I could come up with the name of this nut, and so, to her mind, everything else that I had achieved thus far was null and void.

I continued with the aviary birds in the same vein; capturing their key notes and using them as the basis of my questions. This worked extremely well and the birds all seemed happy to communicate in this way. Mother appeared to become disheartened again. Her furrows reappeared and her arms relocked at the elbows and resumed their crossed position.

Suddenly she took charge. Just as I was about to begin with a particular cockatiel, she abruptly stated, 'Do that one!' Russell opened his mouth to say something, but seeing the expression on his mother's face, changed his mind very quickly. His jaws clamped shut.

I was on my guard now. I had noticed the furrows smoothing slightly on Mother's forehead, and had detected a slight loosening of her elbows. She pointed to a little cockatiel, perched near the back of the aviary. I double-checked, making sure that I had the correct one. I had, so I tried to listen for its sound. Unfortunately, it didn't seem to have one. It sat very still and was silent. 'Aha,' I thought, 'this is why the furrows are smoothing and the elbows loosening.'

So I decided to use the sound of another cockatiel, hoping, since they were of the same species, that it would mean something to this one. It would certainly be a start anyway. I didn't formulate a sentence, I just tested out the sound to see if the cockatiel approved. Gently blowing what I believed to be the appropriate note towards the little bird, I tuned my ears to catch its response. It came. The tiniest little peep with an unusual wheezy quality. Soft, but distinctly there.

I looked closely at the cockatiel and saw that its feathered breast was rising and falling in a slightly harsh manner. There appeared to be a distinct and subtle effort in the movement of those tiny chest muscles. I found myself saying 'It feels just like a chest infection.' That did it. The furrows flew back to the forehead, creating even deeper grooves, and the elbows locked with a resounding crack of the joints. Apparently a direct hit.

Russell explained that he had been worried about the little bird's health lately. And, yes, cockatiels were prone to chest infections. He even went on to name a virus that could affect their throats. He made arrangements for her to be separated from the others for a while, and to get her some appropriate medicine from his little seed house.

We moved on into the house and I staggered my way through a consultation with the dog. Poor Billy had sensed Mother's all-pervading mood, and was convinced that I had come to tell him off.

After Billy, the mother was back up on points. Now, she went in for the kill, choosing one of the three indoor parrots for my final effort. Russell had wanted me to talk to his favourite parrot – a green one, and, I think, Amazonian in origin – because it was so full of life and fun, getting up to all sorts of antics when let loose around the house. Mother was having none of it. 'That one,' she said, pointing adamantly at a smaller African parrot, grey with a red tail.

'Okay,' I replied, sitting down on the floor in front of the cage. I knew she would not be dissuaded from her choice. 'What is it that you'd like to know?' I asked, this time of Mother.

'Why it's so noisy,' she demanded. Russell piped up with the beginnings of a more detailed explanation for me, which is always so much better because it allows me to formulate questions with greater accuracy and understanding. But he gained another shushing clout from Mother for his trouble.

In another room, the father switched on the television and the sound of amplified voices swam through the air and into this, the parrots' room. Almost at the exact moment when the first voice began to speak, the little parrot caught the electronically projected sound and mimicked it. Accurately, but loudly – very loudly. It then picked up the sound of the father whistling, and replicated that, followed by a door closing, before switching back to the television voices again.

Perhaps my ignorance of parrots was a blessing, for this was considered by the household to be normal behaviour. But to me there was an instant recognition of something being very wrong – very wrong, indeed. Although the noises, voices, and whistles were being replicated with remarkable accuracy, on listening to the tone of the parrot itself, I could detect distress. A profound distress. Each time that it imitated a sound, there it was again; a quivering note of upset, alarm, and distress.

I looked around me, around the room. It was full of electrical equipment: a large computer, a hi-fi system, and telephones – one mobile on charge and one walkabout phone, also in its charger. Although none of the equipment was in use, it was all switched on. And, combined with the television, wide screen with stereo amplified speakers – and now, the microwave in the kitchen – it was no wonder that the parrot's feathers were falling out. I was convinced that they were being electronically blasted out!

And such distress. The more I listened, the more I could hear the harsh electronic tone that had become the foundation of its voice; the high-pitched artificial resonance that bound its mimicry. It was almost in a state of shock, if there was such a thing for birds. I presumed there must be since, so often, injured wild birds will not survive any attempts to nurse them back to health.

The bright intelligence so evident in the birds outside in the aviaries, was not here in this little parrot. Every sound that came from the television zapped through it like an electric shock, sending its senses reeling into an alien dimension. I felt myself becoming distressed at the plight of the little bird. If I tuned into its personal hearing frequency, then I, too, heard the voices from the television as something harsh, distorted and screechy; the constant buzz of the computer made my eardrums feel as if they were about to explode; the nerves in my teeth tingled and resonated, sending shock waves through my jaw and down into my neck; my ribs became something that I could feel, with harsh, piercing vibrations shuddering through them, and meeting at a point in my breast bone.

Hang the mother, I thought, turning to Russell and explaining what was happening to his parrot. As I spoke, his innocent young face did not move a muscle, not even to flicker an eyelid. He knew his parrots well and he understood their needs. But he did not know about this. Yet as I explained, he listened, and, moreover, he understood. He declared that he would get another large aviary erected outside as quickly as he could.

This was wonderful news and would be a great help. But I felt that it still might not be enough. The poor little thing was so attuned to electronic frequency now, that it probably wouldn't be able to untune, especially since the neighbouring field sported an electricity pylon, and the garage a satellite dish.

I racked my brains, desperately trying to think of some form of solution. I had to do something – and here and now. For if I didn't, then I doubted that anyone else could, or even would. I couldn't bear to think of this little bird continuing its electronic torture.

My initial, spontaneous thought was to buy the parrot. Then, remembering Mother, I dismissed it. I couldn't think, I just could not think. There had to be something. Just had to be. Out of the corner of my eye, I saw Mother's elbows relax a fraction. Up until now, she had remained silent, but the elbows signalled that she might be building up to her moment of glory.

There is a school of thought that everyone is telepathic to a degree, and this might well be true. For the moment I spotted the elbows shifting, I thought, 'One word – just one word from you, and I'll give you a shushing cuff you won't forget in a hurry!' And, surprisingly enough, she stayed silent, leaving me to my mental searching.

Suddenly I got a flashback – an inspirational flashback. The voice of my music teacher, from way back in my schooldays, pervaded my mind. 'It is *imperative* that you all remember to retune your instruments before you come. Then we won't be subjected to this God-awful row, will we?'

Retune. That was it! Of course, retune the parrot! 'Oh God,' I thought, 'now I'm really cracking up.' I went into one of my mental arguments where my mind seems to become divided and each side offers the benefit of its wisdom to the other half. 'No, no. Not possible' – 'It can be done, I know it can be done' – 'But how? And to what? Retune to what?'

The parrots outside would not do. They were the wrong species and the satellite dish and pylon would be sure to override them in time. 'What? What can I retune it to?'

I had it. 'The trees! Of course, the trees!' Somehow, I knew it would work – provided that the trees had a frequency – a sound. There were plenty of trees outside that would enable the parrot to stay free from the effect of the pylons and the satellite dish. But the million-dollar question was – do trees have sound?

I had nothing to lose, and so I gave it a try.

Getting my mind as still as possible, recalling the sensation of utter peace and calm that I felt when sat beside the tree outside my hotel room, I listened for a sound. A sound to come from the silence. Any sound. The sound of nature.

And it came. Oh, boy – it came. It came as the last dying note of a bamboo wind-chime – the lowest and least audible – the final resonance before the sound tails off and fades away. I held that sound in my chest, hoping that I could keep it long enough for the parrot to register the note. And wishing, above all else, for it to recognise the sound. Hoping that it was a helpful sound, a comforting and homely sound, a stabilising and natural sound for this little bird.

Something happened. I don't know how, or what. But quite suddenly, the parrot shivered. Its chest popped and I felt the same sensation in my own, like an internal expansion. Where my ribs had been sharp and oppressive, they now felt soft and free, expansive and flexible. My ears had ceased their violent humming and now felt still and cool. My fingers had lost their jangled pulsing, leaving my fingertips, once again, calm and comfortable.

I sat still for a moment, surprised and almost breathless, just looking at the parrot. The father wandered back to the living-room from the kitchen, whistling a nondescript tune. The parrot mimicked his whistling. But the sound – the tone – had changed. Yes, still 'parrot'. Still shrill and loud, and delivered with swiftness. But now with such pure clarity, such a peaceful, strong and balanced tone binding them together. No longer the stark, harsh note of distress, but the rich hum of the trees.

Mother was nudging Russell with her toe, prodding him in the thigh. Furrowed and folded, she urged, 'Go on! Go on! Ask her!'

Russell said, 'Parrots are notoriously difficult to sex. It can only be done with a blood test. Can you ask this one what sex it is?'

I answered without hesitation. 'Oh, yes. It's a girl.'

'There you are! Told you! *Now* do you see?' Russell directed his triumph towards his mother, before turning back to me. 'We got the results of the blood test back this morning. They said it's a female.'

16

Geraldine

Nestling into my window seat on the return flight from Jersey, I sipped my plastic cup of tea and looked out at the fluffy white clouds, peppered with sunbeams. 'How peaceful and serene the sky looks from this height', was the fleeting thought that crossed my mind. When one sees clouds so close, they appear so solid, so very tangible. Yet they are really only vapour; vapour that surrounds us all, every day of our lives, although we seem not to notice, or we become so accustomed that we are oblivious to the fact. Here up in the sky was the reminder.

We look up at the rain-clouds as they offload their burden onto our heads and we cry 'yeuch', and run for cover. We sit mellow and relaxed in the summer sunshine, distracted and chilled whenever a stray cloud passes overhead, usually horrified and willing it on its way. Yet up here in this plane it seemed as if I were floating serenely through these clouds. I daresay we were travelling something akin to 300 miles per hour, but with no landmarks outside it was impossible to feel a sense of speed. The vaporous clouds melted around the plane, changing shape and wafting around its wings as it disrupted their stillness.

I wondered what I would have felt had I been able to stick my hand out of the window. Probably just moisture; like condensation, chilled and damp. Yet up here the clouds appeared as huge great tracts of solid white fluffiness.

I was distracted from my clouds by the stewardess handing me the duty free list. I scanned these treasured goodies, giving at least three-quarters of the selection a mental tick. Then I arrived at the section entitled 'allowances', and so settled on a little something for Jackie, a little something for Robert, and, feeling I also deserved a little something, I treated myself to my favourite perfume.

Feeling satisfied with my purchases, having thoroughly scrutinised each of them, I put them in their carrier bag and placed them on the floor between my feet, before turning, once more, to look out of the window. We had dropped in altitude now and the clouds had altered drastically, blending into a uniform greyness, slightly thicker here and there, but very different from the sunlit puffballs visible not ten minutes earlier. 'I guess that's pollution,' I thought to myself.

We were now banking into the landing flight path, not too far from the airport. I nearly always feel a slight sense of despondency after a trip away. I am always very pleased to be home and to be with my own horses again, but I often have a slight feeling of 'that being that', with no idea of what is coming next. I guess that this is not such a bad thing since it leaves plenty of room for surprises.

Robert was there to meet me and we drove home, catching up on the news and gossip. It transpired that my feeling of glumness was completely unfounded. In my absence, we had been approached by more journalists seeking to write articles, and Robert had also arranged for me to do three radio interviews. These had come as a complete surprise and he was quite rightly pleased with his PR endeavours. My despondency was now replaced by trepidation. The words 'Oh crikey' filled my mind.

I had a couple of days in which to prepare myself for the interviews. Robert had requested a list of proposed questions to be sent to me in advance, but I have always found it easier to go in cold. So I occupied myself with the horses and my phone calls instead, and, on more than one occasion, was kept busy chasing Geraldine, my goat, around the young fruit trees in a vain attempt to stop her from taking well-timed swipes at the juicy foliage, and grabbing great mouthfuls for herself.

She is a sweet goat and I have had her for some years now. Originally she was rescued from the meat market – apparently destined for curry – by a lady called Kim who lived at the far end of our village when we lived on the farm. At the time I had a young horse in my yard belonging to a client, and it was this young horse, Misty, who brought about the purchase of Geraldine.

Misty had come to my yard to be 'ridden away'. She was only three years old and, having recently been separated from her maternal friend, was feeling the loss greatly. I felt for her, desperately. Also it does not make for a good start to a ridden partnership if one's horse is full of distress and loneliness. Although her outward and obvious distress had subsided over the first few days, her innerfelt loneliness was still very much a factor. So her maternal friend, Polly, was also brought to my yard. This helped to a degree, but the overriding problem was still there whenever they were separated to be turned out or ridden.

Polly was not particularly pleasant towards Misty, but this in no way distracted her from her adoration of the old mare. I did not want Misty to become completely taken over by her desire for Polly, but neither did I feel that it was beneficial for her to be totally ostracised from Polly's company again. And so another companion was brought into the picture. Geraldine.

Kim's horses and her goats seemed to get along very well, and when I rang her for advice on where to get a goat, she offered the immediate solution. She had just bought two young goats, and said that I was quite welcome to come and choose either of these, or one of three others that she was prepared to sell to good homes.

As I entered Kim's goat field, I was given no time to choose. Geraldine raised her head from the grass, bleated loudly, and scampered over to me. I found this surprising for I had no connection with goats at all, so it wasn't as if I carried the scent of them on my clothes. I was very flattered however, so, choice made, home we went in the car. This arrangement Geraldine seemed to find most satisfactory.

I have the philosophy that if animals want to be with me, then they choose to. So, disregarding Kim's advice to keep Geraldine shut in for a few days, I left her to roam and familiarise herself with her new surroundings. She immediately skipped and frolicked into the tack room, and around and behind the feed bins, realising very quickly that she could get their lids off. Then she bounded up to the top of the stacked hay bales and back down again, before springing up onto the wall surrounding the yard and skipping deftly along its rounded top in true Alpine style. The horses were mesmerised but she paid them scant attention as they snorted down their noses at her. She then turned her attention to the dogs, taking an instant liking to Snuffi who reciprocated with great glee, licking her nose and wagging his tail with the ferocity of a turbocharger. And off they went together; round and round the yard, up and down the haystack several times, and back round the yard again.

I was delighted. Geraldine was obviously very happy here and was staying of her own volition. When she had all but worn herself out, I took her round to the stable that I had prepared for her. She followed me in and I showed her to her supper which she tucked into straight away. I felt that she had had enough excitement for one day and intended to introduce her to Misty the next morning. So, leaving her to enjoy her meal, I went out, shutting the stable door behind me.

Immediately, poor Geraldine became very upset. She ran to the door and jumped up at it, bleating frantically. So I went back in to her and stroked and soothed her until she settled again. I left her once more, and yet again she expressed immediate distress, tearing round the stable in panic and bleating loudly. I obviously needed to take alternative measures. Geraldine was not happy alone.

I thought for a moment or two, toying with the idea of bringing Geraldine into our house for the first night. While this idea appealed to me enormously, I doubted that I could convince Robert to be equally as delighted at the prospect. I abandoned that idea and decided that it would, perhaps, be best to put her in with Misty now. After all, there's no time like the present.

Geraldine followed me round to Misty's stable and came in with me to meet her. She stood still to receive the ministrations of Misty, who breathed on her; first on her ears and the top of her head, then on her neck and shoulders, then along her spine and down her back legs. I watched Misty, not sniffing at Geraldine, but blowing on her; expelling great breaths of air onto her, then pausing to inhale several short shallow breaths, pausing again and breathing out, pushing her breath onto Geraldine's silky black coat. All of this took some considerable time on Misty's part in her role as 'blower', while Geraldine, adopting the lesser role of 'blowee', stood patiently.

I watched this ritual with fascination. I had seen so many horses do it, but had never stopped long enough to really observe and understand. Whenever horses meet, there is always a phenomenal amount of blowing at one another, the emphasis always being placed on the outward breaths, and the inward breaths being far less detectable. I wanted to ask Misty what she was doing exactly, but the pair were so engrossed, I felt it better to stand quietly and not interrupt. When they had finished, they both went to Misty's haynet, Geraldine pulling strands from the bottom and Misty from the middle. Each seemed happy with the other, relaxed and settled.

I locked up the yard and walked the short distance to our little house feeling really happy. Geraldine was wonderful, a delight to have around. Snuffi had taken to her instantly, and she to him. Misty had unquestionably accepted her into her home and Geraldine was pleased to have company. Only Robert to convince now. 'Perhaps I'll blow on him,' I mused.

I wasn't sure just how much Geraldine would alleviate Misty's need for Polly. There was little point in assuming that Misty would forget the older mare altogether, but I hoped she would find a togetherness with Geraldine that would placate the greater percentage of her yearning. Polly was, in fact, not at all nice to Misty. She would call to Misty whenever the pair were separated, but as soon as they were reunited, she would pick on the younger horse. She would flatten her ears and make glaring faces at Misty, deliver a sound chomp or two, and chase her around their paddock. Misty would become upset and respectful, but was never put off by Polly's rejection. If anything, it seemed to make her more determined to seek an attachment.

I kept an eye on the budding relationship between Misty and Geraldine over the next week. While Misty was out in the field with Polly, I would let Geraldine romp around the yard, reuniting horse and goat when it was time for Misty to come back in.

During that week something quite strange began to happen. From what appeared to be the beginnings of a close friendship, blossomed something quite different. Misty began to treat Geraldine in the same manner that Polly treated her. She adopted the same face-making and threatening gestures with the odd bite here and there. Whenever Geraldine sat curled up in the stable, Misty would chase her. None of this was connected with feeding times. It was like watching Misty metamorphose into Polly; one could have easily substituted Misty for Polly and Geraldine for Misty, watching the antics in that stable.

Misty knew that I found this behaviour most unacceptable, just as I did when Polly victimised her. Consequently, she behaved much better towards the little goat whenever I was around. When I wasn't, I would often hear Geraldine's great loud bleat sending the message 'Help!' echoing round the farm. By the time I'd reach the stable, the sound of my running footsteps would have acted as deterrent enough, for Misty would always appear angelic in contrast to poor Geraldine's alarm.

I hoped that all this would be temporary, a mere blip in my plan. But deep down I knew that it would not pass. Misty had quite definitely adopted Polly's behaviour, placing Geraldine firmly in her old shoes. I had become very fond of my goat, and although Kim had assured me that I was welcome to return her, I decided to keep her. So I moved Geraldine to a different stable, caring too much for her to see her so victimised. From then on she lived amicably with Arnie – provided that she didn't touch his breakfast or evening meal.

However, I remained fascinated by Misty's role reversal. I pondered and puzzled over it but could not put my finger on the reason behind it. Why? Why should a victim become a bully? Surely if one has experienced victimisation, the memory alone should be enough to make one compassionate and choose not to inflict the same treatment upon others.

I sat in the kitchen of our little barn conversion, mulling over this idiosyncrasy that still played on my mind, unable to put my finger on it.

That afternoon, a selection of highlights from a three-day event was being televised, and I decided to make time to watch it. It was excellent coverage and showed each competitor sailing around the big-well-designed cross-country course. Skilled tactical riders steered their horses over imposing and complex obstacles: drop fences, combination fences, water jumps, huge open ditches, and stacked log piles; each having chosen their route with care, riding with accuracy and precision.

Something leapt out at me that afternoon. The so-called 'bogey fence'. A fence which, on first appraisal, appeared so straightforward – especially for those skilled riders and highly trained horses, our nation's elite. Yet so many of them came to grief at that fence. So many, one after the other, and all in similar ways, each seeming to follow in the exact same faltering footsteps of the previous competitor. As news of this fence filtered back to the start, the following riders were warned, and consequently rode with ever greater dexterity, compelling their horses to take heed of their instructions and pay attention. They too faltered or came to grief, through no fault of their own.

This truly was a bogey fence. But why? My mind was crowded with ideas and hypothetical reasons and explanations. But I rejected each in turn. None of them afforded me the complete answer; each still left me unsatisfied in my quest for the true reason.

Geraldine continued to be an integral part of our four-legged family. She would accompany me on short rides around the farm, or go off with Snuffi on expeditions to the pheasant pens, where he would stand mesmerised, nose pressed to the wire, tail wagging, while she perused the brambles and woodland vegetation. When they chose, they would come home together, pausing en route to frolic with the piglets, until Mavis the breeding sow expressed her disapproval.

One day in late summer, Geraldine declined her walk to the pheasant pens and also ignored my invitation to accompany me on a ride across the stubble fields. She mooched around the yard looking decidedly sorry for herself. Later that afternoon, I asked Robert to take a look at her, thinking that she was perhaps more closely related to sheep than anything else, and therefore his husbandry skills would serve her best. He found the problem in a flash. Her udder was sore, inflamed and swollen. She had started to produce milk and, for some reason, had incurred an infection.

I had the fortune to know an excellent homoeopath and it was she whom I contacted now for advice on treating Geraldine's condition. She recommended a choice of two remedies, both of which I had in my first-aid cupboard. She named the one for which she held the greater preference. I thanked her profusely, but for some reason, I decided to let Geraldine choose for herself.

I decanted one tablet of each remedy onto its own clean teaspoon and offered them to Geraldine – one in my left hand and one in my right. She looked at both spoons and paused. Then she reached her nose out to the spoon on the left and sniffed a couple of times, almost imperceptibly, before doing the same to the one on the right. She then repeated the procedure, pausing over each tablet in turn to take tiny delicate inward breaths.

Suddenly, and without further ado, the teaspoon in my left hand disappeared into Geraldine's mouth; tablet crunched and swallowed, spoon in danger of following. She had quite literally pounced on it and I had a job to wrestle the spoon from her. She bleated, soft and low in her throat, licking her lips with swift movements of her tongue. She bleated again and stretched out her nose to the empty spoon. I knew she meant 'more'. I offered her the right-hand spoon, still complete with tablet, but this she rejected without so much as another sniff. Two soft bleats now. 'More.'

She followed me to the tack room, waiting beside me while I took the lid off the little bottle. I gave her another tablet which she devoured with such eagerness that I nearly dropped the bottle. And another one, swallowed with equal enthusiasm. I knew this wasn't goat greed, but just to make sure, I offered her a fourth. She snorted, sending the tablet shooting onto the floor. Then turning away, she left the tack room and went to make herself comfortable on Arnie's rug which lay folded up outside his stable.

I felt compelled to sniff for myself the two little bottles of tablets. I then unscrewed the lids of the other remedies that I had and sniffed carefully at each of those in turn. They all smelled the same. No matter which one I sniffed, to me they all smelled exactly the same. I also had the supposed advantage of being able to smell a far greater quantity of tablets than just the two that Geraldine had been offered. And yet my nose could detect no difference between any of them.

I looked over at Geraldine lying on her cosy bed and said, 'I can't tell the difference.' She responded with a soft chuckling sound, low down in her throat. There was clearly no wisdom in my sense of smell.

There was little wisdom in my continuing to chase Geraldine round the young fruit trees at the present moment either. She was much too fast for me and way too tantalised by her tastebuds to pay me any great heed. So I left her to her pruning and went into the house to make myself a cup of tea and roll a cigarette in preparation for my first radio interview. I didn't plan to actually puff and slurp over the airwaves, but I did need to calm my nerves while I was sitting by the phone waiting for the interviewer to ring me. My nerves were not helped by the fact that I knew Robert and Jackie would be lurking in the kitchen, hovering over the radio.

The call came and I was serenaded by interlude 'musak' before I was introduced on air. Then came the voice of the interviewer. I could hear him quite clearly. 'And now we have, live from Gloucestershire, a lady who claims she can talk to animals. Ha-ha!'

My back bristled at his twanky metallic voice. It was not so much what he had said, more the tone in which he had said it.

Then he said my name. 'Mrs Mackin? Are you there, Mrs Mackin?'

'My name is Mackay, actually,' I corrected.

Now he sounded flustered. 'Oh, er, sorry. I do apologise, Mrs Mackay.' He went on to ask me a series of questions, all of which were superficial and basic, affording me little opportunity to answer with the clarity and depth that I would have liked.

It was all over relatively quickly, and it was only as I replaced the receiver that I realised I'd been interviewed by an extremely sceptical and highly disbelieving man. I also realised that, by the end of the interview, this man had become polite and almost interested. I felt this to be quite a triumph, all things considered.

I did the other scheduled interviews and they seemed to go fairly well, with the exception of the final one which was another radio interview, this time for the BBC World Service.

I was required to drive to the local BBC studio where my part in the interview was to take place. I set off, but my worries about being late caused me to take a few wrong turnings here and there. Circumnavigating yet another roundabout, my mind swam with the horror of arriving only to discover that the whole thing was all over, and I'd missed it. I dropped down a gear and sped off the roundabout, determined to be on time.

I found the studio and signed myself in, taking a seat in the reception area and trying my best to appear relaxed. I gazed at the pictures on the walls, photographs and posters, all pertaining to the radio station and meaning little to me.

After what seemed like an age, the thick door to my left swung open. It looked like the door to a vault, with a great metal doorknob and a metal keypad panel glaring out from its stark white exterior. A young man popped his head round and called me through. I left my seat and followed him, the great vault door swinging shut behind me, unaided.

I trailed the young man down an all-white corridor to a T-junction. The corridor was lit by evenly spaced fluorescent strips which cast their harsh artificial light over the walls. There were many more doors, also white, inlaid in white-glossed frames, heavy metal doorknobs standing out from each. Two sported small rectangular peephole windows, inlaid with wire-mesh fire glass. These were strategically placed but too high up for me to see through.

I was shown into the interview room, situated just off to the right of the T-junction. The young man briefly introduced himself. 'Hi. My name is Paul. This is where your interview will take place. Put these headphones on. When the clock strikes midday, you'll hear a loud buzzer. Press that switch and you'll be connected to the World Service. Okay?' His last word was not a question. It was one of those loose words flung in to adorn the end of a sentence. 'I'll be back later,' he concluded, throwing this comment over his shoulder as he left via another stark white door.

So there I was, sitting in a big, black, quilted swivel chair, a pair of headphones dangling from my right hand, staring at the most enormous piece of electronic equipment I had ever seen. It would not have looked out of place in the cockpit of a World War II bomber. Small circular lights flashed orange, green, and red at me. And switches. There were thousands. They were everywhere.

'Which one did he say? Was it that one? Or that one? Oh, my God!' I didn't know. I surveyed them again. Disregarding all others, I looked at the mass of switches and lights to my right. Mentally narrowing down the selection, I ended up with a choice of two. Tentatively I stretched out a finger, then thought better of it. 'I have to wait for the clock,' I reminded myself.

That clock. That plain white circular clock with its simple black hands and black numerals, hanging on the plain white walls, illuminated by the fluorescent strips that buzzed overhead. The ticking of that clock and the buzzing of the strip lights were the only sounds to break the silence. I had felt confused from the moment I'd entered that all-white room with its buzzing lights, switches, and ticking clock.

I had three minutes according to the clock. 'Three minutes in this room,' I said to myself, feeling more tortured than ever. I felt very strange. I had noticed a ladies toilet on my way down the corridor, so I decided that a short walk and a visit would be better than just sitting here for three minutes. I twisted and turned the door handle, checking and double-checking, making absolutely certain that I could get back in without being locked out. I glanced again at the ticking clock. Two minutes now. 'How long does it take to go to the loo?' I thought.

I sped off and returned with one minute to go. Walking back into the room definitely made me feel very strange again. Strange, confused and jittery. I felt my eyes begin to blur and blink furiously. Resuming my position in the well-greased swivel chair, I said a silent 'thank you', glad that this was radio. The way that my eyelids were shooting up and down over my eyeballs with the speed of light, I would be in trouble if it were television.

No sign of Paul or anyone else for that matter. No sound other than the ticking of the clock and the buzzing of the lights. I placed the mammoth headphones on my head, trying to halt my batting eyelids long enough to fix a still focus on the hands of the clock. The headphones were enormous, the earpieces ending somewhere either side of my neck. Thirty seconds to go. I fiddled frantically with the adjustor on the headset, getting them to the smallest size possible before replacing them on my head.

The buzzer sounded. It came from nowhere. Loud and accusing. I nearly fell off my chair. The harsh sound reverberated around the clinical white room – and around me – sending shock waves through my eardrums and my teeth. My eyes stopped their blinking, more through shock than anything else, and bulged painfully in their sockets. I might possibly have felt less concerned had my headphones fitted, but they were still dangling around my jaw.

Then I remembered the switch. 'Oh, crikey! The switch! Was it that one? Or that one?' I couldn't think. My mind was buzzing and whirling. I just pressed any one, flicking it down with a spare finger, my others fully occupied, grappling with the headset.

The buzzer stopped. I could hear crackling in the earpiece that I held firmly to my left ear. The right earpiece had positioned itself under my chin and seemed happy to stay there. Then I heard the voice of a man. He introduced himself as being from the World Service and asked me if I was Nicci Mackay. 'Phew.' I heaved a huge sigh of relief. I let my eyelids bounce up and down over my eyeballs a few times. My temples pulsed like a food processor. 'Yes!' I yelled at him. At least I had found the switch and the World Service. Thank God for that.

My relief was short lived. For the more this man spoke, the more his voice took on the resonant buzz of the fluorescent lights. I don't recall what he said and at the time I barely understood one word. I believe he was trying to put me at ease prior to going on air. He then advised me that he could hear me quite clearly and that I had no need to shout.

My hair was now starting to lift off my shoulders and crackle with static. As I crossed my legs my clothes sparked, and the lights on the panel in front of me flashed and danced in time with the voice of the interviewer. The clock continued to tick and the strip lights continued to buzz. I was connected all right. I was so connected to the World Service, I thought I was going to spontaneously combust!

I received a small shock from the metal arm of my black quilted chair, and my hair floated around my blinking eyes with gay abandon. The right-hand earpiece was sending vibrations into my tongue and throat, making it very difficult for me to formulate any words at all, let alone a lucid comprehensible sentence. My temples continued their impersonation of a food processor. 'I can hardly understand these questions,' I thought. 'I must sound like a complete idiot.'

I was given a brief reprieve as another horse whisperer was introduced – a man from Australia. As I listened to this man with his deep, slow, gravelly voice, I felt my heightened senses subside a little. He was being interviewed in the open air of the outback. This was a blessed relief for me. The more I listened to his voice, the more I felt myself returning to some semblance of normality, becoming comprehensible myself at last. By the time I was asked my last couple of questions, I could not only understand, but I was able to answer in a reasonably lucid fashion.

Interview concluded, Paul reappeared. 'All right?' he said, popping his head around the door – again, not a question to which he expected an answer, just a word used to fill a gap.

I half-toyed with the idea of saying, 'Well, actually, no. Your room is like the inside of a ghetto blaster, and if you spend too much more time in here yourself, you are quite likely to be struck by lightning on a stormy day!' But he did not grant me the time. He was off, leading the way back down the corridor to the large vault-like door. He punched in a series of numbers on the keypad and it swung open.

I stottered through, back into the reception area, which, mercifully, had windows letting in natural light. Signing myself out, my hand wobbled and shook. Instead of my normal signature, I left a scratchy spiky mark resembling a dying spider trailing two legs. My hair continued to waft around like tentacles, lured towards the computer screen on the receptionist's desk.

I staggered back to my car, gasping great lungfuls of outdoor air. Despite the slight flavour of carbon monoxide, it was bliss when compared with the air inside that stagnant studio environment. I received an electric shock off the car door, plus several more as I completed the drive home, hair swirling wildly. On arriving, I got out of the car to open the gate into our yard, taking great care not to touch the car door where possible.

Tilly, our young grey thoroughbred mare, was in the paddock alongside the gateway with her inseparable friend Kerfuffle, a Welsh pony, and Geraldine. I paused for a moment to smell the sweet air which was fragrant with honeysuckle. Wrestling with my hair, I smiled at Tilly. She started to trot over to greet me. She got to within about 50 feet of me and stopped dead in her tracks. Huge great snorts flew from her extended nostrils. Her eyes grew large and fixed, and her heart began to pound in her chest. She would not come any closer. She snorted at me, blowing and prancing, but she would not cross that invisible 50-foot barrier, and neither would Kerfuffle, nor Geraldine.

I had apparently turned into a monster. Tilly continued to spin and twirl, blowing great loud snorts at me down both nostrils. Kerfuffle and Geraldine stood still and stared, alert and wary. It was so obvious that they could feel, see, and hear my static state, despite the distance between us. What they could sense from me, I knew, was that same deranged static confusion that I, too, had felt on walking into that stark white studio room. I was still me – someone they had known closely for years – but right now I was surrounded by bouncing frequency waves. I was enveloped in my own personal magnetic cloud.

I retired to the bathroom in search of normality. A bath and a hairwash would help enormously, I hoped. I was a little concerned by the possibility of electrocution so I tentatively tickled the bathwater with one fingertip, just in case. All seemed well so I climbed in.

Lying in the bath, revelling in the delicious sensation of hot water adorned with perfumed bubbles, I shuddered to myself at the recollection of the day's events. The interview experience paled into insignificance for me, when compared with the blatant horror displayed by my four-legged friends. I might not have been so concerned had the response come from only one of them. But all three? That was too much.

'What on earth must I have looked and felt like to the animals!' I wondered, 'let alone sounded like to the listeners of the World Service?' I shuddered again and groaned to myself, making a mental note. 'From now on, I will conduct all interviews in the open air!'

Tilly's expression remained clear in my mind. No matter how much I tried to alter my train of thought, her image would not budge. Then I recalled another time I had witnessed such a goggle-eyed expression on a horse. This one had been a seasoned hunter who, one day, had refused point-blank to enter a woodland path, quite out of character. His facial expression had portrayed the same startled alarm. Other memories flashed: of a cat that had inexplicably flattened its ears at someone, of dogs that bit certain people, of the remarkable incident with Geraldine and the remedies and spoons, of Geraldine and Misty, Misty and Polly, and that bogey fence. It was all linked, I knew it. Very linked.

Geraldine and the tablets suddenly seemed so simple. They were both different remedies, each having a different energy, sending out a different message. She had let the message of each remedy drift up her nostrils, up into her highly attuned brain. Messages that my brain had been unable to read. She had 'read' each remedy and had chosen the one that she knew would suit her condition. And it had. Just those three tablets had cleared her problem.

It was my message that she and the two horses had read just now. 'Danger! Electricity pylon on the move!' Hardly surprising that they had kept their distance and looked so startled and horrified.

The answers to long-standing mental puzzles were just beginning to fall into place.

I thought back, stilling my mind, replaying memories in slow motion, looking for detail – detail that I had missed. Misty blowing all over Geraldine; Tilly blowing at me. It was this blowing that struck such a chord in my mind, the images of which I held in my head like cinematic stills.

'Blowing. Why blowing?' I mused. I picked up a handful of bath bubbles. They engulfed my entire hand, creating an undefined mass. Holding them up to the light, I could see rainbow colours swimming through the delicate transparent surface of each perfumed bubble. I blew on them, gently at first. I watched them move, becoming elongated and stretching away from my pushing breath, their fine rainbow colours swirling, spinning and stretching with them as their shapes changed. I took another breath. This time I blew harder, sending wisps of loose bubbles flying away across the bathwater to land on the taps. I blew again, harder still. This time with a real clearing force. The bubbles surrounding my hand responded. More wisps flew. Some bubbles burst, their existence dissolved in a flash; others slid across my fingers and along my arm.

There! Where had previously been an amorphous mass of pretty translucent bubbles, was now the palm of my hand – made pink and clean by the bathwater, but clearly visible. My hand.

'That's it!' I shrieked out loud, slapping any remaining bubbles against my forehead. 'Of course! That's it!'

I leapt, Archimedes-like, from the bath and dried myself swiftly and vigorously. Flinging on an assortment of distinctly non-fashion items, clashing in colour and unflattering in style, I charged downstairs and scrabbled through the video cassettes underneath the television. Finding one labelled 'horsey vid', I slid it into the recorder, watching the screen with avid anticipation. The screen cleared to show . . . *Rugby*? – Scotland playing Wales, accompanied by the excited voice of Bill McLaren.

'*Aaargh!*' would best describe the noise that involuntarily leapt from my throat to mingle with his commentary. Murder One! Robert was shortlisted for assassination!

I sped through the tape on fast-forward, zooming through football highlights, athletics, rugby, more rugby, and a short section of a film. But no horses. Not a horse in sight.

Racing out of the house, I clattered across the moat bridge, breaking stride to address Mrs Miggins, and cannoned into the office, causing poor Jackie to leap from her chair in astonishment. 'Where's Robert?' I asked urgently, my excitement overshadowed by my desire for assassination.

'Up at the workshop, I think,' replied Jackie, fingers still poised over her keyboard.

I shot up to the workshop where I found Robert making a door for our indoor school. 'Tapes! I need tapes! Without *rugby* on them, or *athletics*! I need horses!'

Robert, concentration still firmly fixed on the bolt he was attaching, very nearly vaguely said, 'I don't know'. But when he reached the 'd' of 'don't' he glanced at my face and changed his mind. 'Try that box over there,' he said, waggling a screwdriver and cocking an eyebrow in the direction of a large cardboard box that we had neglected to unpack.

I rummaged, then rummaged some more. Eureka! Robert's life was safe for the time being. Clutching three tapes, I flew back to the television. I shoved in the first tape, one of Desert Orchid winning the

Gold Cup. There was some excellent slow motion footage. I watched closely. So, so closely. And there it was!

As Dessie approached each fence, he checked his own stride, unaided by jockey. With each slowed down extension of his forelimbs, on the last stride before take-off, came the inward breath. With the gathering and collection of his great flashing white hindquarters, came the expulsion of breath – just as he made himself airborne, he breathed *out*, emptying those magnificent, heroic lungs and pushing his breath before him. It was this breath that gave him his power. The power to sail over the huge fences. The power to clear the way ahead for him.

I swapped tapes, to the one with the bogey fence. I hoped fervently that it was still intact as I slid it into the machine. One hint of rugby and I would run for an axe. Thankfully the event came into view, accompanied by the voice of Lucinda Green.

I watched those riders come to grief, one after the other, each following in the footsteps of the previous competitor. I watched closely as each rider approached, steadying their horses, Lucinda's concerned commentary clearly audible over the sound of the horses' hoofbeats and heavy breathing. One by one they tripped and scrambled, sliding, some to a halt. Others even fell.

I watched the one horse who broke the mould. I watched the little bay thoroughbred speeding across the ground towards this, the bogey fence. I watched the rider check him slightly with a light firm hand on the rein, before urging him forward. I saw that little horse take a big swallowing inward breath as his greased and booted leading foreleg touched the ground in front of the fence. And I saw him expel an enormous breath ahead of him at the exact moment that his sleek muscular quarters gathered to propel him off the ground.

He sailed over that bogey fence – without breaking stride or rhythm – earning himself a 'thank you' pat from his rider, who slackened his hold on the reins as they sped off up the track towards the next obstacle.

I watched that section of tape again and again, just to make sure. It was there. All there. My mind was working overtime. I went to the kitchen to make myself a cup of tea and let my mind swim back; back to the days when I did housework in the old people's home. Pictures entered my head of a sideboard, a book, an ornament, all covered in dust; a thick layer of dust, disguising the sheen of the mahogany sideboard, obscuring the title of the book, and binding enshrouding cobwebs to the figurine.

Many times I had blown on these articles and the dust had dispersed, just as the bubbles covering my hand had dispersed, just as the puffball clouds are dispersed way up in the sky when the wind blows. Many times I had wiped a finger across these dust-covered items leaving a clear strip; revealing the rich wood of the sideboard, the gilded letters of the book's title, the bright glazed china of the ornament. But where had the dust gone? It was still there – on my fingertips – defined and visible. A smear of thick dust that I could rub and spread across two fingers, maybe even three. But it was still there. There to stay until I washed it off – too thick to disperse by blowing.

And suddenly I understood. Suddenly it all made sense. I took my tea through to the sitting-room and thought back to Misty blowing on Geraldine when they'd first been introduced. Misty blowing on Geraldine's head, back and legs, as though she'd been covered in a layer of dust, or shrouded by a coating of bubbles, or been obscured by a thick white vaporous cloud.

Misty had blown until she'd *found* Geraldine. She'd blown until Geraldine's true identity had become distinguishable from mine, from Snuffi's, from Kim's other goats, from the meat market, and from the haystack. She'd blown until she had known who and what Geraldine was. Just as Tilly had snorted great cannonball shots of air at me, trying to find my identity in that cloud of static, in that harsh magnetic energy that pulsed, sparked, and vibrated all around and through me. She had snorted and blown from the edge of my magnetic forcefield, a good 50 feet away, unable to find me – a clear definable me.

And Polly. What of Polly? I sipped my tea and allowed memories of Polly to flood my mind. Staid, stout old Polly with the attitude, full of her own will, and reliable in it, unchanged in mood and temperament for over 25 years. What dust had she gathered? What cobwebs had clung to her down through the years? And what quantity of her thick historic dust had rubbed off onto Misty every day that they'd spent together? What amount had been pressed into Misty with every bite, every shove, every glare? How much had been absorbed through Misty's nostrils, imprinting her mind, each time she'd reached out her nose to take tentative sniffs to appease Polly's rejection of her?

It was Polly's invisible, grey swimming cloud of influence that had swamped Misty, that had tainted her view of life – and her view of Geraldine. Just as the grey cloud mass had enveloped my plane on its descent to land from Jersey, blocking out the rays of the sun. Just as each faltering horse and rider had left an invisible mist of alarm, shock, disappointment, and pain, to intermingle with the expressed emotions of the ever-growing number of onlookers who'd crowded round that bogey fence. That fence, which had become ever more disguised and distorted to the vision and senses of the horses – by an incomprehensible, but tangible, mass.

A mass of energy.

17

A Photographer Calls

My thoughts were suddenly scattered in all directions, as were the video tapes, the ashtray, and my cup of tea, by a barrage of dogs. Besieged by pink licking tongues and furiously wagging tails, I tried as best I could to lift myself from my forced prostrate position on the floor and answer Jackie. She had found the suspense far too much to bear so came over to the house with all the dogs.

'Tell all then,' she said, plonking herself in an armchair.

'Well, this is amazing!' I said, hardly beginning to explain myself properly, and waved the Desert Orchid video tape at Jackie. 'You see, it was Tilly really, she started me off when I came home. Then I remembered Misty and Polly. Then, after my experience in the BBC interview room, things began to take shape so I thought I'd look at these tapes and just see if I was right. It's incredible really, you can actually see it on the tapes!'

Jackie, quite accustomed to my ways now, merely said, 'Hold on, I'm going to need a cup of tea and a cigarette and you'll have to start from the beginning. I can't keep up.' I followed her to the kitchen and made us both a cigarette. Whilst Jackie made the tea I began to regale the story of Misty and Polly. The kitchen door flew open, aided by Robert – a somewhat dishevelled Robert.

'It's nearly 3 p.m., the photographer will be here in a moment,' he exclaimed as he shot through the kitchen and vanished into the dining-room. My mind was blank, all my thoughts washed clean by the word photographer. I looked at Jackie, poised stock still, holding the lid of the teapot three inches away from the pot; her mind was blank too. Robert reappeared clutching a pair of clean but crumpled trousers.

'What photographer?' we both enquired simultaneously.

'The one from the German magazine. You know, I told you . . . didn't I?'

No was the answer but that seemed completely irrelevant. Suddenly my loose 'casual attire' became my worst nightmare. 'Oh, my God, look at me!' I clutched at the sides of the extremely baggy, pale grey tracksuit bottoms I had flung on after my innovative bath. They had been Robert's but had somehow succumbed to the rigours of the washing machine and were now a most peculiar shape and too short even for me. A knock at the front door took a stream of barking dogs flooding through the house. I was still frozen, rooted to the tiled floor. Jackie sprang into action, placing the lid swiftly in place on the pot and said, 'Tea is ready.' Robert leapt into action, running swiftly to the hall and up the stairs, completely ignoring the poor photographer standing on the other side of the door. So, too, did I. We both frantically rummaged through a pile of clean clothes on our bed, Robert desperately searching for something pressed, myself for anything less horrific.

'Whose are these?' asked Robert, holding aloft a pair of Jackie's brown tailored corduroys.

'They're Jackie's,' I said. But he was not to be deterred, frantically shoving his leg into the trousers and plonking himself on the bed so that he could get a good tug on the trousers. 'They won't fit you,' I said in disbelief.

''Course they will,' replied Robert, now tugging at the waistband lodged around his knees.

I flung his slightly crumpled 501s at him, telling him they were fine, no one would notice that they were slighty creased, and anyway, it was fashionable. Anything to stop him from tugging poor Jackie's cords completely in two. Finally, he conceded and wore his own trousers. I settled for a clean pair of jodhpurs and a T-shirt and we both composed ourselves with a couple of deep breaths before going downstairs to meet the photographer.

Jackie, always at her best in a crisis, had made him comfortable in the living-room and was indulging in polite conversation over tea. We made our introductions. Rodger Schmitt was a freelance photographer commissioned on behalf of a German family magazine to take a series of photographs which would accompany an interview I had done some weeks earlier. He was very charming and explained clearly the type of shots he was looking for. It was very apparent that he was skilled and knew his profession well. As he explained, I found myself cringing inside. I am not at all confident with this sort of thing and the more professional the photographer, the more I feel out of place and self-conscious. Robert was quite relaxed, being very photogenic himself, and he discussed potential sites in and around the garden for the inevitable family shots which were prerequisite for this particular magazine. Rodger was eager to get on, though I tried to ply him with more tea and some of Robert's home-baked biscuits to delay the inevitable. He politely refused and picked up his large camera bag. It was neatly packed to the hilt with an array of cameras, lenses, film, light monitors and various wires of which I had no comprehension.

We made our way up to the top paddock where Arnie, Ben and Herbie were. Rodger was great, chatting to me and trying to put me at ease. Unfortunately it didn't work and I found myself becoming ever more self-conscious, probably because I was aware of what he was trying to do and somehow that made it worse. Also I was about to become the victim of my own discovery. As we entered the field, the horses, Herbie in particular, became very aware of my own uneasiness and they knew exactly how I was feeling so immediately decided that they too did not want their photographs taken by Rodger, and rather than coming closer together for the shots, decided to move further apart. I knew that this gave credence to my revelation and felt almost compelled to explain to Rodger. I decided against it, especially as Rodger was under the impression, though I'm not sure from where he got the idea, that I could make horses jump through hoops blindfolded. Unfortunately, right now I couldn't even make them keep still and look at the camera. I could hardly blame them, though, the fact that I was so uncomfortable with it made them extremely suspicious. After a while things seemed to fall into place and Rodger felt satisfied with the rolls of film he had taken.

As we strolled back down the drive towards the house, Rodger inquired as to its history. I explained as much as I knew but also found myself looking at the property afresh in the bright afternoon sun. It was beautiful: the young fruit trees had grown a good deal since we had first arrived; the grass in the paddocks was beginning to take on a slight tinge of brown; baked by the sunshine, the honeysuckle and wild rose bushes glorious and bedecked with healthy blooms; the comfrey that took root by the office now taller and stronger than ever, its huge green leaves fanning out like a climbing frame for Jack in the tale of the Beanstalk. The pansies in the wooden tubs around the yard bright and glorious despite Geraldine's appetite; and the house itself so serene and peaceful with its tiled roof and expanding wooden beams. Every time I looked at the house, I fell more and more in love with it. Every time I came back from a trip away, the house seemed more wonderful than when I left. We walked across the moat bridge and the sound of our feet on the wood brought the greeting of Mrs Miggins from underneath the bridge. This was her afternoon resting place, cool, quiet and peaceful, and sheltered from the heat of the sun but lit by the beams of light that shone through the gaps in the wood. She was never alarmed by our passing overhead and she would just chuckle in her throat, a cross between a 'cluck' and a 'beep'.

I took Rodger around the side of the house into the garden, the large garden that had sprung into glorious life over the summer months. The flower-beds had once been full and absolutely blooming with flowers of all shapes and sizes, but over time they had withered and died. But now with the lawns mown and the beds weeded, it looked clean and refreshed, ready to start anew.

Jackie, Robert and I had chatted about the garden, hoping to make some time to plant and tend it as it should be tended, but life had rattled on at such a pace we were lucky to find time just to sit and enjoy the garden as it was.

Rodger spotted the ideal site, according to the light and direction of the sun. 'Over zer, by ze flower-bed. We can put ze table and chairs zis way, and a dog or maybe two here und here.' He pointed to the sweeping curve of the lower end of the garden where it bordered the two bottom paddocks, one of which contained 'The Munchkins', four miniature Shetland ponies and in the other paddock four more equine inmates, Harry, Jackson, Dillon and Freedom.

'But first, before you change your clothes, I take shots of you and Robert on ze grass wiz ze dogs, just here,' said Rodger, pointing to the exact spot in the middle of the lawn.

'Change my clothes! What, again?' I thought, sitting down on the grass beside Robert with Foxi and Snuffi in front of us. There we sat, grinning inanely at each other, trying to hold hands in a relaxed and completely comfortable manner, whilst Rodger went about his work. Not easy, I can tell you. Foxi and Snuffi were great, rolling upside down with not a care in the world. Jackie stood out of view hanging on to Fizz and her two remaining puppies, Pie and Sam, both of whom were destined to stay with us for ever it seemed. All three were straining at their collars, desperate to join in.

'Zo, and now we can come here and do ze lunch in ze garden,' said Rodger, quite enjoying himself. He and Robert carried the pine table to Rodger's designated location and placed it exactly where Rodger indicated. 'No, no. Left just a little, forward two steps and now back one, ja, is great just zer. Nicci, you need to change and wear a little something for lunch, something light and for summer and we can put a bit of food und wine on ze table.'

'Okay,' I replied, going back to the house. Robert seemed to get off scot free in his crumpled 501s. 'A summer something,' I said quietly to myself, racking my brains with alarm at the prospect of my limited wardrobe.

Thank heavens for mother, who for my birthday had sent me some loose silk trousers. I had never found the appropriate occasion on which to give them an outing and they had remained tucked at the back of my drawer. 'It seems your time has come,' I said to them as I rummaged for my pink silk T-shirt. After all, I spend my life talking to animals, why not to a pair of trousers. I put them on and discovered that they were incredibly long, but having little else in the way of choice, I hoiked them up and scurried downstairs in search of elastic bands that I could put around my ankles, thinking this was a brilliant flash of inspiration. I went to the front door with the idea of a quick dash to the office and back, but just as I got down the stairs I heard some rather alarming crashing coming from the kitchen. In the kitchen I found Robert, leaping from one practically bare cupboard to the next, clutching a pyrex salad bowl.

'He wants food on the table,' exclaimed Robert, 'and wine with glasses and crockery and cutlery.'

'But we haven't got any food.'

'I know,' said Robert, 'but you take the crockery and cutlery and I'll . . . I'll make a little something!'

Thrusting a stack of plates and glasses at me, he then dived into the fridge grabbing a wilting third of cucumber, half a limp lettuce and two tomatoes. I didn't dare ask, so I hobbled out into the garden hanging on to my trousers with one hand and clutching the necessary table decorations with the other. I laid the table, wishing that we had gone shopping, and tottered back to the kitchen having twice tripped over my trousers. Robert was busy spooning the leftovers from last night's supper – which Jackie had thoughtfully mixed with dog food and put in the dog-food bucket, ready for the dogs' evening meal – into the pyrex salad bowl. Seeing the look on my face, I didn't know whether to laugh or cry.

Robert said, 'Don't worry, it'll be fine, trust me; I'm a doctor!'

'But what if he wants us to eat it?' I asked in horror, to which Robert replied, 'Well . . . we'll worry about that later,' and continued to spoon with conviction. Leaving him to it, I found an empty wine bottle and filled it with water. I also found a very dry segment of cheese stuck to the cheeseboard and one solitary bottle of beer. I took them out into the garden and arranged them on the table.

Rodger asked, 'Can we haf zom vine in ze glasses?'

'Eh, yes,' I said, so I poured water into each glass then topped it up with beer, giving it just the right colour for a white table wine. At this point Robert appeared, striding across the lawn carefully holding his pyrex salad bowl which he deposited on the table with a flourish.

'Oh, very nice,' said Rodger, seeming extremely pleased as the lunch table seemed now complete.

'Just a little something I rustled up,' said Robert nonchalantly. I looked at the 'salad' and couldn't believe my eyes. Robert had carefully sliced the cucumber and tomatoes, even grated a carrot from goodness only knows where, to create the most wonderful looking 'salad' surrounded by the lettuce leaves which by some miracle were now standing to attention. On close inspection it was because they were firmly wedged into the dog-food base which Robert had sculpted into a mound shape and disguised beautifully. We sat in our allocated chairs as Rodger instructed, lifting our wine glasses as if in a toast. Then Rodger had an inspirational idea. 'Could we perhaps have a horse in the background?'

Freedom, Jackie's little bay thoroughbred, had caught Rodger's eye. He was leaning over the fence from the field into the garden, his pretty little 'Bambi' face alight with intrigue. He was always compelled by photographers and cameras and never shy about having a close-up photograph taken. So Robert and I downed glasses and Jackie went to get a headcollar and bring him into the garden. Unfortunately, to do this she had to let go of the dogs who had all smelled their supper and were in no way fooled by a grated carrot and a few lettuce leaves. They crowded around the table, eager with anticipation. Jackie led Freedom through the small wicket gate from the field into the garden and took off his headcollar. He wandered across the lawn taking mouthfuls of the more succulent grass and Robert and I raised our glasses once more and at Rodger's signal clinked them together and said 'Cheers'.

All hell broke loose. Freedom took off around the garden squealing and bucking, rearing and spinning. The two puppies, Pie and Sam, darted off, running for cover; Foxi dived between my legs just as I stood up from my chair and trampled all over the excess length of my trousers; both Fizz and Snuffi seized the opportunity to make a grab for their supper as everyone's attention was diverted. Robert spotted them and set about defending his salad from their slavering jaws. 'Get

down, get down! Freedom, whoa, steady Freedom! Sam, Pie, here.'
The still of the summer afternoon was shattered by a barrage of
instructions. Freedom's antics had a catalystic effect upon Harry,
Jackson and Dillon who all joined in and began galloping around their
field. Freedom consequently galloped around the garden with ever-
increasing speed, Jackie in hot pursuit with a headcollar, Robert still
clutching his dog-food salad, me trying to keep my trousers on and
untangle myself from Foxi at the same time, and Rodger hiding
behind a tree.

Finally, peace and order were restored. Freedom was back in the
field with the others, grazing peacefully; Sam, Pie and Fizz were back
in their stable, Foxi and Snuffi in the kitchen and the salad neatly
arranged on our plates. Rodger, happy with the light, focus and
content of the shot, had one final request: 'Could you just be chatting
to each other as you pass ze cheese.'

I looked at Robert as he passed me the cheese, hoping he could
think of something to say as I definitely couldn't, and to his eternal
credit he did.

'Oh, by the way, Sue rang this morning. She has accepted the
Horten-Smith's offer for the Moat House; oh yes the other thing is Fizz
is pregnant again.'